Developing Quality Computer Systems

A. Coogan

NCC Blackwell

MANCHESTER·OXFORD

British Library Cataloguing in Publication Data

Coogan, A.
Developing Quality Computer Systems
I. Title
005.1

ISBN 1-85554-250-1

Published by NCC Blackwell, 108 Cowley Road, Oxford OX4 1JF, England.

Editorial Office, NCC Blackwell Limited, Oxford House, Oxford Road, Manchester M1 7ED, England.

Typeset in Times Roman by H&H Graphics, Blackburn; and printed by Page Bros, Norwich.

ISBN 1-85554-250-1

Acknowledgements

This book is based on years of experience, not only personal experience but that of numerous friends and colleagues. I learned much while employed in a variety of roles at Glaxo Holdings and am grateful to many of my former colleagues for their help and opinions over the years. Among those I should like to mention by name are John McCarthy and Paul Nathan who provided much valuable advice in the areas of computer operations and implementation, helping me to see these neglected topics in a new light. I am also grateful to Mick Spelman and Peng Sai Cheng for their advice on systems development and to Mike Hird who was always keen to discuss quality issues.

At the Information Systems Quality Association and the European Security Forum, I was able to meet others with an interest in making quality and security an integral part of systems development. Both of these organisations are making a valuable contribution to the process of demystification and provided me with useful, stimulating ideas.

Preface

When you write a computer system, do you ever ask yourself – "Is this system going to be legal?". Most of us were taught that the chief aim of all systems design is to produce something which satisfies the user's requirements. How many users actually stipulate that a computer system must comply with the law? In my experience, they are few and far between. Yet, if a system is to be a quality system, one truly "fit for the purpose", surely this is something we should be concerned about.

Legal considerations are but one of many aspects of systems development which are not given the attention they deserve. Until recently, university courses in systems development rarely spent much time on quality and security issues. To date, most innovation has been in the areas of systems analysis and design. Over the past decade, methodologies such as SSADM and LBMS have been developed and improved and are now widely used. CASE tools have relieved us of some of the donkey work and now help us make sure that the diagrams we produce are consistent. Object orientation has enabled us to approach systems development from a new angle. But the emphasis of this innovation has mainly been to enable the established systems development process to become faster and more efficient.

These developments are necessary since computer systems are frequently much more complex than they were twenty years ago. But a number of well known problems remain. Getting the requirements right is one of them. How many systems, however well they function, have to be amended within weeks of implementation because they do not really do what the user wanted? They may perform perfectly according to a systems analyst's understanding of the requirements but that is a small consolation. Of course, most computer systems will have to be amended at some stage in their life. It is generally accepted that you can alter a system much more easily if it is well-documented. Yet it remains a neglected area because the provision of up-to-date system documentation is not always treated as an essential component of the project.

A quality system is sometimes defined as one which conforms to its original specifications and performs as expected. This means, not only does it do what the user wants it to but also that there are no nasty surprises – things which the user did not think of or which were taken for granted. Therefore, the quality of a computer system requires more than traditional analysis and programming, however well done. The project manager needs to ask wide-ranging questions about the system's role and the implications of its introduction. Users may not be aware of these issues.

Then there is the actual process of systems development. It is right to delegate responsibility to staff but it is all too easy to use delegation as an excuse for permitting slapdash work. Controlling this is only possible if the system is developed as a group effort and everything is subject to the scrutiny of others. Years ago, some programmers were allowed to treat their work almost as private property, masterpieces whose arcane workings need not trouble others. When they moved on, others had to puzzle over these masterpieces when they had to be amended. The day of data processing artisans, who jealously guarded their trade secrets, is over. Quality practitioners have argued for years that, if all work is reviewed, there is far less likelihood of errors remaining undetected. If others can understand a program when it has just been written, there is reason to hope that the same will be true in years to come.

This book concentrates on such matters, which are not normally dealt with on training courses and which are sadly lacking from many training manuals. It focuses on practical issues faced by systems development management and staff who want to ensure that the systems for which they are responsible are well written and that all the implications of the system are fully considered. Where most books on systems development concentrate on the design and construction of computer systems, the emphasis of this one is on the earlier and later stages. There is a large literature on systems analysis and design methods and methodologies – a small selection of which is given in the bibliography.

Using the well-established method of the systems development life cycle, which will be familiar to most development staff, this book incorporates quality assurance techniques into everyday systems development. It asks questions designed to concentrate minds on all the implications of whatever phase of the process is being undertaken. Only two assumptions are made. The first is that all projects will be managed with a project plan, standards or other guidelines. The second is that all work produced during each phase of the life cycle will be subject to review.

The contents are not confined to any specific systems development techniques, methodologies or programming languages. While they are most readily accessible for those with experience of business projects, they are also suitable for degree level students who have acquired systems development skills and whose courses emphasise the practical side of computer applications. In addition, 'in-house' development is no longer the only kind of systems development. Computer packages are increasingly used, sometimes with modification and sometimes as a component of a larger system. A hard-pressed department may not be able to satisfy all of its users so outside resources have to be brought in. The life cycle can be used as a means of supervising a third party development and ensuring that work is done to a high standard.

Everything produced within each phase of the life cycle is subjected to two kinds of scrutiny. The first is a detailed look at what is going to be produced, in which the developer will ask himself or herself just what is needed to ensure that the work will be complete and thorough. The second is the review, in which the work will be checked to see that it is complete, free from errors, consistent with earlier phases of development and complies with standards. The review also takes a broader view and looks at the relation between the document in question and the systems as a whole.

The life cycle chapters are the central part of the book. In each chapter, all the documents which may be required to complete the phase are listed and explained with a section on what should be considered in order to produce each document. Following this, there follows a section on what should be considered when reviewing the documents.

Checklists are always phrased as questions since they are intended to stimulate thought and self-questioning. Of course, they cannot be completely comprehensive. The variety of computer projects is huge, no two computer departments are the same and, besides, systems development is always changing. You should be ready to adapt them where necessary to match your way of working. If used properly, they will provide real assistance in writing and reviewing systems documents. Initially they may generate more work, but it is better to be aware at an early stage rather than to pick up the pieces when things go wrong.

The emphasis is always on practical action rather than theoretical knowledge. This book seeks to help systems development staff in asking the right questions and in finding solutions so that they can use their expertise more effectively. It is not a substitute for training in and experience of systems analysis, design and programming skills, nor for the other essential ingredients of a successful project – good management, initiative, imagination and talent.

Unfortunately, this book will not be of much use to those who thrive on chaos – people for whom emergency late night working is the stuff of life. They are the authors of their own predicament. Having extricated themselves from near disaster, they congratulate themselves but do not pause to examine their own working practices. I have known project managers who have approached operations staff on the day a system was due to begin live running, and announced that it had to be handed over there and then with no documentation, training or scheduling. This is asking for trouble and some will go so far as to admit it. But, when you tell such people that it is possible to break this cycle of incompetence, they lapse into a kind of fatalism, declaring that this is what inevitably happens in the real world. This 'real world' is a myth and anybody who works in an environment where such thinking prevails will soon see improvements if this book is used conscientiously.

Contents

1 The quality life cycle

The concept of a systems development life cycle is well established. It is a convenient way of dividing a project into phases, each of which is a distinct stage requiring different skills, frequently performed by different staff. This in itself makes project planning and control easier.

The life cycle given here is designed to be comprehensive, flexible and to enable quality to be built into the work. It is comprehensive in that it can be used for projects of all sizes and of differing degrees of complexity. It is flexible in that it accepts that a small project, perhaps a minor subsystem added onto an existing one, may not need the whole range of activities and documents described here. A few key documents kept up to date through the life of the system are identified but apart from that project managers should be eclectic and decide what they need for a particular project. The life cycle is no substitute for good management but will assist managers to decide what they need to do during each phase, make their plans and see that what is produced meets their standards.

This life cycle differs from others in two ways. The first is that it is designed to enable project managers to build quality into systems. The second is that its scope includes a number of activities which are not normally dealt with in systems development methodologies. For example, how do you deal with an applications package which will form part of the complete system? What should you do if you think a prototype might be a good idea? How should you deal with security issues? All are part of systems development and cannot be overlooked because your methodology does not mention them.

Completion of each activity in the life cycle is always determined by a review. Therefore some kind of output which can be inspected and understood by others is always produced – it might be a written document, a diagram, a program listing or a set of test data. If quality is to be built into the system, you need something tangible which can be assessed and verified independently.

THE PHASES OF THE LIFE CYCLE

There are six phases in all, taking the project from the initial idea to post-implementation.

Initiation

This phase begins with the recognition that there is a need or a problem which may be solved by a computerised solution. This has to be defined in broad terms appropriate to the working environment, for example, if it occurs in an accounts department it should be seen in that context. After examining different solutions, a recommendation is made as to whether or not the project should go ahead.

Definition

The idea for a computerised solution is now converted into a well-defined functional specification, the system proposal. This must show not only how the original problem will be solved but also state quite clearly any requirements which are not going to be met. With user agreement to this specification, the project is truly under way and must be planned, with time-scales, costs, resources, training requirements, all identified in broad terms. A quality plan is also recommended here.

System specification

The system proposal is used as the starting point for a thorough analysis of the requirements, with all the data and processing identified. In turn, this is used to define a detailed system specification which describes in precise, unambiguous terms everything that the system will do. Once reviewed and agreed, this document becomes the central document for all further development and remains in force for the life of the system. It must therefore be kept up to date.

Programming and testing

Starting from the detailed system specification, program specifications and a system test plan are prepared. This is followed by all coding, program testing and system testing. Training plans and user and operational documentation should also be written during this phase, although they may be modified during the user evaluation.

Evaluation and acceptance

Now the users can decide if the system really does what is required. The system test results may be enough, although the users will probably insist on their own testing. They will also review the user documentation. If the system is going to be run by computer operations staff, their manager must review and accept operational documentation.

Implementation and training plans should be agreed by all concerned. Everyone who is going to use or operate the system when it goes live must be trained now.

Post-implementation

The system has now been implemented in accordance with the plan and has ceased to be a development project. Any further changes are dealt with under change control procedures for live systems. However, a review after the system has been in operation for a time should be carried out to ascertain how well it is performing and to discuss possible alterations.

Roughly speaking, a methodology such as SSADM is most useful when applied to some of the activities in initiation and definition and all of system specification (*see* Figure 1.1). Some methodology techniques and diagrams are also useful elsewhere, for example as an aid to training.

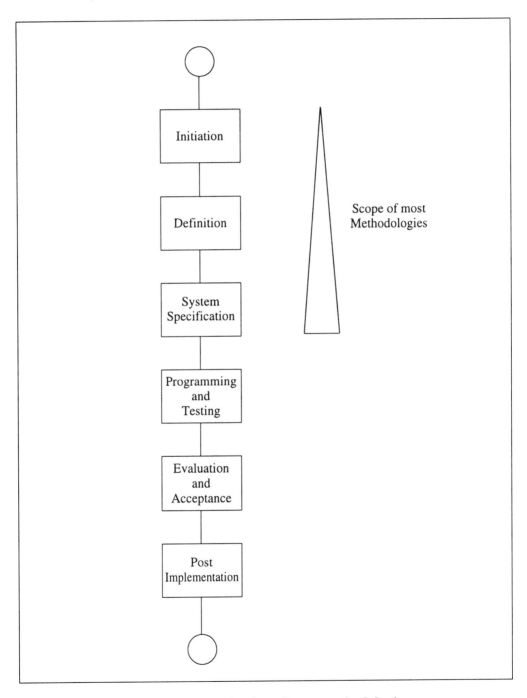

Figure 1.1   Application of most methodologies

STRUCTURE OF THE LIFE CYCLE

Each phase of the life cycle is structured in the same way, albeit with some minor variations. The main sections are as follows.

Phase initiation

The phase is triggered off by some event, examples being:

- a decision by the project manager that sufficient information or documentation is available to begin this phase;
- the completion of the previous phase.

Activities and documents

Each activity has as its aim the completion of a document for review. Therefore all activity is seen in terms of creating or revising a document and checklists are given to help decide what the contents should be. The form of the document will often be the subject of company or departmental standards or of the methodology used by the project team. Recommendation about the form of documents is therefore only given in a few cases.

Review

Further checklists are given to assist in the review process. These concentrate on the things which should be looked for by those conducting the review. For example, you should be able to trace the contents of a document produced during the definition phase back to the initiation phase.

Anyone working on a document should be encouraged to look at the checklist which is going to be used in the review as well as the one designed for preparing the document. The object of the review is improve quality in general and to make sure the document will be as good as it needs to be within the framework of the current project.

End of phase

This is the event which determines that the phase has been completed. Typically, this will be:

- a satisfactory review of a key document;
- user agreement to a key document.

REWORK

The object of the review is to weed out all errors, inconsistencies, ambiguities and other defects from the document under review and to make sure it fulfils its intended purpose. The first version of a document will frequently need some revision. The activity will not be considered complete until the project manager agrees that the document is good enough. Rework, then, is a cyclical process although, in most cases, a document will only be revised once after a review, see Figure 1.2. Reworking will also be needed when circumstances change, for example when a new requirement is demanded, perhaps during a later phase of the project. The latter situation can be tricky to manage. Appendix 2 'Managing change' describes how it can be kept under control.

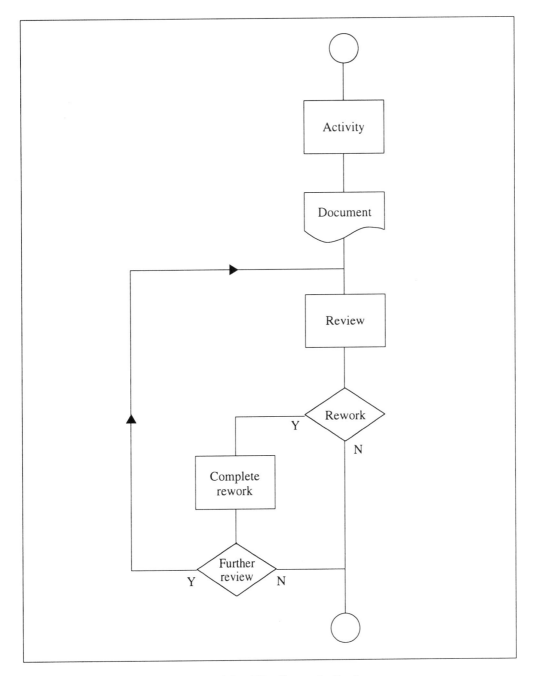

Figure 1.2   The Rework Cycle

Examples of circumstances where reworking will be needed are:

- the user decides a feature of the proposed system is not acceptable or that alternative or additional facilities are needed;
- an inspection of the document finds that it contains defects which must be remedied.
- it has been previously agreed that the document should be presented as a draft.

It may appear that the emphasis on rework will enable some people to perform slapdash work in the knowledge that it will be sorted out by others in a review. Experience shows that such individuals are rare and are soon discovered. Most people take pride in their work; indeed you are more likely to find that it is hard to persuade people to accept that their work could be improved.

Nor should the contents of the life cycle ever be used as an excuse for not performing tasks with care and initiative. If, for example, it is discovered that the checklists are not appropriate in some way, project staff should be encouraged to voice their concerns rather than follow the rules blindly.

The introduction of word processing, desktop publishing and on-line development tools makes the actual physical process of rework quite easy. The same applies to document changes after the system has been implemented. There really is no excuse nowadays for failing to keep documentation up to date.

DOCUMENTS VS DELIVERABLES OR PRODUCTS

The output of every activity should be something which is tangible evidence that the activity has been done and can be read and reviewed. 'Document' conveys this idea whereas terms such as 'deliverable' and 'product' do not.

Take a program for example. A programmer may state that he has tested it and may have spent much time doing so. A busy project manager may be tempted to accept this statement or merely to try out one or two tests. This falls far short of verification or review. The product is indeed a tested program but a review would need at least a test plan with the anticipated results given and every test ticked off as complete and, preferably, certified as correct by someone other than the programmer. The more the project manager is under pressure, the greater the need for clear evidence of what has been done. In this example, well-presented test plan and results will make review much easier.

A document does not have to be a written document; diagrams are often used, especially during the system specification phase. Data flow diagrams, data models, entity life histories, user role/function matrices are all used instead of written documents or to supplement them. Their logical presentation makes them easier to review. Take a user role/function matrix for example as shown in Figure 1.3. It is much easier to get a clear picture of who performs each function from a diagram such as this than from a written description. This does not mean that a review can be omitted or made less rigorous. Good presentation makes it easier to spot any defects and to check for consistency with other diagrams. The presentation of the example given in Figure 1.3 highlights one potential problem area. Only the warehouse manager can check stock levels. What will happen if he is away?

This book could not hope to cover all diagrams produced by all methodologies. Some are discussed, particularly during the system specification phase, and some general points are made on how to construct your own checklists.

User Role/Fuction Matrix

Project/System	Author	Date	Version	Status	Page 1
SALES	AC	27/1	1		of 1

User roles \ Functions	Authorise Orders	Authorise delivery date	Produce sales documents	Produce invoices	Inquire about orders	Monitor progress of orders	Record payment	Inquire about customer status	Check stock levels
Sales Director	X	X				X		X	
Depot Manager	X					X		X	
Sales Staff			X		X			X	
Chief Accountant					X				
Warehouse Manager		X				X			X
Accounts Staff					X		X		

Figure 1.3   User Role/Function Matrix

RESPONSIBILITIES AND MANAGEMENT STRUCTURE

Each company has its own idea about where the computer department fits into the company structure. Some are subsidiary companies, others are virtually autonomous having to treat their colleagues as customers and charge them for everything. At the other extreme, a computer department may exist entirely at the whim of a director with everything paid for out of his or her budget. On top of this, each computer department has its own local management structure and views about staff responsibilities.

The life cycle can be used in any working environment but, as you read on, you will notice that a departmental structure is assumed in many of the examples. It is always assumed that there is a dedicated project team responsible for a systems development project under the supervision of a project manager. The latter reports to a systems development manager who is in overall charge. Within the computer department, there are also computer operations staff who are responsible for running live systems and data management. Being an enlightened department, there are also quality and security specialists. The reason for this is that it is easier to think of responsibilities in terms of people who have a role to play in the project, even though they are not actually members of the team. Thus, where the project manager has to think about the production cycle of a new system, one important source of information and the target readers of relevant documents are computer operations staff.

A hierarchical structure, appropriate for a project team within a systems development department is given here but only for illustration, see Figure 1.4. The job titles refer only to functions. This should not be taken as a recommendation for any specific departmental structure. The checklists in the life cycle can be adapted to suit your own departmental and company structure. The 'in-house' scenario given here will not apply to software companies but the relationship with users and computer operations will be much the same – it is just that they will be in different companies.

Whatever structure is used, it cannot be emphasised too much that the life cycle is not a substitute for good management, planning and project control. All those working on a project must know what their individual responsibilities are. You may find that no-one will admit to being responsible for something, generally something they would rather not do. Readers of Clifford Stoll's *The Cuckoo's Egg* will be familiar with the phrase "not in my bailiwick". If this happens, the traditional solution of "kicking it upstairs" may be all you can do.

Here the systems development manager is head of department and responsible for getting the project under way and generally supervising the project manager. The project manager is in charge of virtually every other aspect of the project.

Systems Development Manager

– agreeing the terms of reference;
– deciding what documents need to be produced during the initiation phase;
– reviewing initiation documents;
– setting any overall project standards;
– recommending to the user whether or not the project is viable and worth proceeding with;
– reviewing and approving the project plan;
– deciding when the project is complete.

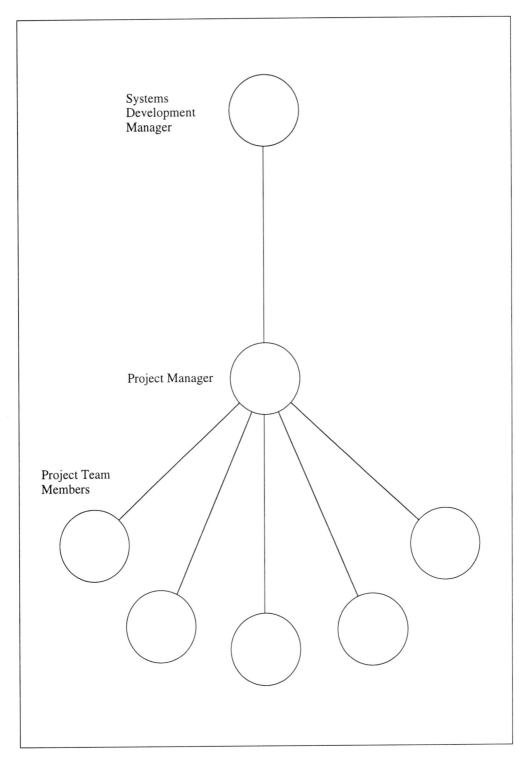

Figure 1.4   Project Team Hierarchy

Project manager

- writing the project plan;
- establishing channels of communication with users and others not directly involved in the project;
- reviewing documents;
- allocating of tasks to project staff;
- providing guidance to project staff, ensuring that all are familiar with the life cycle and know what is expected of them;
- day to day management of the project;
- deciding whether a phase is complete or that rework is necessary;
- managing changes;
- identifying areas where the life cycle could be improved.

Project staff

As well as systems analysts and programmers, the project team may include users, operations staff at different stages of the project working as team members.

- carrying out tasks in accordance with the project manager's instructions and guidance;
- understanding the requirements of each activity and its place in the project;
- participating in review sessions.

Users, computer operations and others

- agreeing the extent of their involvement in the project and naming individuals with specific responsibilities;
- taking an active part in the project where this has been agreed;
- data management;
- providing expertise and advice when this is needed, for example regarding current operational security;
- making clear decisions when required.

Quality Assurance

- quality measurement;
- assistance with reviews;
- quality statistics.

Security

– all computer security issues, standards and practices.

The above deals with all the normal activities of a project. Sometimes, though, a new issue will arise and it will not be obvious who is responsible. For example, it may be necessary to tell a subsidiary company to send data for the system. Will the project manager or someone in the user department take charge of this or should the request be passed up the company hierarchy? This is not important in itself. What is important is that the problem should be identified and someone in the team made responsible for finding out and reporting progress. If it is accepted that someone has to be made responsible for every activity and steps are taken to make sure the activity is actually completed, no difficulty should be encountered.

PROJECT MANAGEMENT

The life cycle given here is appropriate for most systems development projects. Sometimes, though, it may be difficult to decide whether it is appropriate. As a rough guide, it will be easier to introduce the life cycle for new systems or subsystems than it is to amend a badly documented system. The questions and answers given here may provide some guidance.

Is the system a brand new one, a complete rewrite of an existing one or a major new subsystem for an existing system?

The life cycle should be used in all these cases. Although it is easiest to introduce it for a new system, the only time you will meet much difficulty is if you are replacing an old system which has little or no useful documentation. Some time will have to be spent on finding out how it works because it is likely to be the starting point for deciding what the new one should do. Also, some data from the old system will probably be transferred to the new one.

Can the life cycle be used when making amendments to an existing system?

This may occur when a new system makes changes to an old one necessary or simply as a matter of changed requirements. Whether or not the life cycle can be used will depend on the state of documentation. If a certain number of key documents are present and up to date, namely system specification, program specifications, operations and user documentation and, preferably, system proposal and statement of user requirements as well, it will be easy to introduce the life cycle.

Problems will occur when a system has been allowed to grow without being properly controlled with unspecified amendments and 'quick fixes' or the documentation is out of date or does not exist. If this happens, it is worth considering bringing the documentation up to date as a prerequisite to making the changes but this may not be possible. It may not be worthwhile bringing a system's documentation up to date, especially if the changes are minor and the system is due for rewriting.

On what other occasions might the life cycle be dispensed with?

The quality life cycle approach imposes rigour on the development. If it is not used, the possibility of errors arising are increased and more work may be required in the future. The only times it can reasonably be dispensed with (apart from minor amendments to old, badly documented systems) are:

- – a genuine emergency when something has to be done without planning to avert a crisis;

- – when improved technology, such as case tools, means that some of the procedures given in the life cycle are redundant .

An example of a 'genuine emergency' could be a payroll system which needs a change of a field size so that staff are paid. If the problems arises on pay day, the life cycle might be dispensed with in order to prevent a strike or to save the company from being sued by irate employees.

The introduction of new technology may reduce work and dispense with laborious checking. Before all review by human beings is abandoned, care should be taken to make sure the development tools do everything the humans did.

The new system is going to be a package. Is the life cycle relevant here?

Applications packages are frequently used for payrolls and other systems which are common to many users and whose function is partly defined by legal requirements or government regulations. Of course, you may just wish to evaluate a package, install it and leave it at that. Generally, though, the package will interface with other systems. A payroll will probably interface at least with a personnel system and an accounting system. The users may request extra reporting, not provided by the package, and the package will have to fit into whatever menu system the company uses. Therefore, the package will have to be supplemented by 'in-house' development.

The life cycle can be used if you are evaluating and installing a package alongside your own systems development as a single project. The suppliers should provide enough documentation to let you integrate their product, in which case the workload for systems analysis and design will be much reduced. Nevertheless, the life cycle will help you to integrate it and to address requirements not met by the package. It will also assist you in making up for shortcomings in the package. You might find that the documentation provided with the package is not very helpful and decide to write your own. That, too, is a life cycle activity.

How should the project manager deal with activities which are not given here?

A manager may decide that the project requires some activity which is not covered in this quality life cycle. For example, a system may have to be accessed by an overseas company at a later date and the project manager does not know much about it. So, he has to consider what effect it will have on the project. Will it be necessary to consider equipment compatibility, special security options, systems availability? Someone will probably end up with the task of writing a report on the subject.

When such activities are needed, the project manager should consider the following when planning.

- • What is the aim of the activity?

- • What limitations (for example, Time constraints) will be imposed?

- • What document will be produced?

- What standards will be used in preparing it?
- Who is it intended for?
- What criteria will be used to judge its success?
- To which phase of the life cycle does the activity belong?

It can then be dealt with as part of the project plan in the same way as any other activity. Where no standard exist for a document, the form should be given in the terms of reference for the activity.

What is the bare minimum which can be used?

If a project is small or a system is being amended, only a relatively few activities may be needed during each phase. This is especially true if familiar ground is being covered. Let us say that a subsystem is being added to an existing system, with no links outside the current system, perhaps to provide some extra reporting. Here a scaled-down life cycle should be considered. It would be foolish not to make sure that the requirements were spot on, so the initiation phase should not be overlooked.

INITIATION

Statement of requirements costs/benefits report.

DEFINITION

System proposal, project plan.

SYSTEM SPECIFICATION

Amendments and additions to the system specification.

PROGRAMMING AND TESTING

Amendments to current program specifications, new program specifications, system test plan, program test plans.
    Program coding, program testing, system test.

EVALUATION AND ACCEPTANCE

Implementation plan, amendments to user and operations documentation.
    What if we are looking at a small amendment to a system, for example, the size of a single data item might have to be increased? The user department may not be even aware that anything needs to be done. However, the temptation to merely change one or two programs should be resisted. As will be seen later, some system documents describe the current state of the system and must be kept up to date. For a change to a data item, it may be necessary to change the system specification, program specification, design and coding. Where was this data item first mentioned? We need to trace it back through the development process to find out where its size was first defined. The other important thing

to be considered when making such an amendment is to inform all who are affected, for example, owners of other systems which access this one, as shown in Figure 1.5. This is dealt in more detail in Appendix 2 – Managing Change.

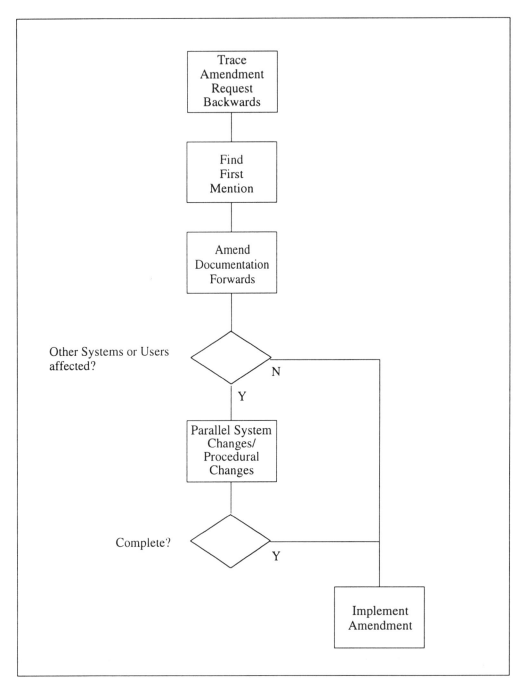

Figure 1.5   Change Management

Does one phase have to end before the next begins?

It is neat if you can complete one phase before going on to the next but this can conflict with good project management. If staff are available, why not give them something useful to do? This is especially true during the latter stages of the project. Why wait until all the programming has been completed before beginning work on the documentation for users and computer operations?

The difficulty lies when there is pressure to go ahead with the system because of urgent deadlines when user agreement has not yet been obtained. The project manager must decide what is the likelihood of changes being requested. If changes are needed, not only will the document in question have to be altered but all subsequent work will have to be reviewed and probably altered as well. If forced to go ahead before agreement has been obtained, all the project manager can do is try to build an element of contingency into the project plan to enable some reworking to be done as soon as a decision has been made.

THE LIFE CYCLE WITH THIRD PARTY DEVELOPMENTS

The life cycle is a useful means of controlling the activity of outside companies which write applications systems for others. Some of these companies provide a very high standard of system because quality is more than just a slogan for them. Some will be accredited to ISO 9000, the internationally recognised standard for I.T. Quality. Others will appreciate the need for some form of review with their customers during development if only to make sure that the system is still going to reflect the original requirements. Unfortunately, however, there are some software companies which seem to prefer to work from the most sketchy of requirements, as though this was evidence of their abilities. The result is often a badly written, error-prone system which is at best a reflection of the vaguely assessed requirements. Needless to say, such a system will soon need to be amended, but who is going to maintain it? It might provide a lucrative contract for the company that wrote it or give the computer department a collective headache for years to come.

If a software company claims that it can write systems without standards, methodology, documentation and reviews, or if it says that this would make the system more expensive or delay it, you have every reason to be suspicious. The fact that the company has experience of similar systems to the one you want does not mean that it will understand your particular requirements. You could well end up with the same system as the last customer.

What can you do to ensure that a bought-in system is written to a high standard? The life cycle can be used to achieve this aim in two ways. In the first place, you can make sure that the end product is well-written, well-documented, easy to use and maintainable. You can do this by using the checklists to make sure that the requirements include things that the users might not think of such as defining a specific speed of response. Why not have a system which is written to your standards?

You can also make sure that the process of developing the system is good enough and that it is implemented in a way acceptable to both users and computer operations. Insist in advance on all the key documents of the life cycle being written and reviewed. Protect your interests by appointing somebody with the same experience as a project manager to take part in these reviews, or delegate the responsibility where specialist knowledge is required.

This shadow project manager should report on progress and make sure, for example, that there is proper consultation, that programs are written to standards and so on. In other words, he or she represents the interests both of the users and of the computer department who will one day be responsible for looking after the system. Why be satisfied with work which is of a lower standard than you would permit? A good software company will gladly cooperate with such arrangements, since they mean that you are helping them to get the system right. In the case of a company accredited to ISO 9000, you will probably have little to do. Those cowboy companies which complain or refuse to cooperate should be asked to saddle up and ride off into the sunset.

REVIEW

How should reviews be conducted?

The best formal review technique is the software inspection developed by Michael Fagan. If properly conducted, the Fagan inspection method is very thorough and will normally uncover a high number of defects. The statistics which quality assurance specialists derive from it provide a valuable means of improving the quality of future work. The method requires training, especially for the moderator, the person who organises and conducts the review. It also needs planning and preparation although each review is normally limited to two hours or so. Perhaps more than anything else, a change of thinking is required in which it becomes quite normal to submit one's work to the close scrutiny of others, including those who may occupy a much less exalted position in the company hierarchy.

If you decide to use the Fagan Inspection Method, you should introduce it with the assistance of quality assurance experts. Although there seems to be a lot to learn at first once you have a little experience the method is actually not at all difficult. In the longer term, the number of defects found will fall as staff learn to look more critically at their own work.

The Fagan Inspection Method is best used when quality assurance staff are available to advise and to use the statistics from the inspections as a means of improving quality. For example, they may draw attention to a way of working which could be improved by training. If you are not in a position to use the Fagan Inspection Method, then it is still worthwhile using as many of the features of the method as you can, such as asking inspectors to take different viewpoints and look for different types of defect.

A less stringent approach may be all that is needed in many cases. Let us say that a programmer has written a test plan for a program. It should be reviewed but, if a single program test plan is defective, it is not so important as, a system proposal. The sooner any faults in the system are discovered the better and reviews are therefore particularly beneficial if conducted during the initiation and definition phases, especially on key documents such as the statement of requirements and the system proposal.

Planning the reviews

Whichever method is used, the project manager should make the reviews part of the project plan from the start. Nor is it enough merely to pencil in to the plan that a review would be a good idea and leave it at that. If you accept that reviews will improve quality then it is obvious that a task is not complete until the review and any subsequent rework has been done. The plan should include the following information for each review.

- When will reviews be carried out?
- What documents will be reviewed?
- What will the documents be compared with, e.g. Source documents, checklists, standards?
- What review techniques will be used?
- Who will manage the reviews?
- Who will take part in the reviews? In the case of Fagan inspections the moderator can choose whom to invite, although this is normally from a fairly small number of possible candidates.
- Who will decide whether the document is ready for review and using what criteria?
- What follow-up is permitted after the review?
- How will rework be checked?

When it come, to the detailed planning of a review, three further points should be considered.

- Why are we conducting this review? What are the goals we hope to achieve? Error detection, consistency with a source document and meeting standards are some obvious aims applicable to most documents but you might want to be more specific. The aim of a review of a user manual may be that you want to make sure that someone with no computer expertise or knowledge of computer jargon can use the system. Why not make sure that at least one of the reviewers can look at the manual from this point of view?

  There are checklists provided for reviews in the life cycle chapters. See also the general points on review given below under "what should the review look for?"

- What are we going to compare the document against? As well as checklists and standards for contents, there will often be one or more source documents. There are also some criteria which are true for most documents, for example – is the document readable? Of course, different standards of readability will apply to a report written for a user and to a piece of program code, but the principle is the same.

- how will the results be communicated? Obviously the specific results of the inspection will be used to improve the document under review but they must be written down clearly to an agreed format. Jottings in the margins are not enough. Also, general lessons may be learnt from a review which will benefit others, so some of the results have to be communicated to a wider audience. It goes without saying that the review must be seen to be fair and as a way of benefiting everybody and never as a way of drawing attention to the failings of others .

What should the review look for?

You will find a checklist for each life cycle document in the following chapters. In addition, there are some general questions which you can ask of almost any kind of document, including diagrams.

It will help during the review if each inspector takes a different viewpoint. Let us say we are looking at a system proposal. This should show how the project team proposes to provide a computerised solution which will enable everything in the statement of requirements to be met. From it, we need to be able to produce a detailed system specification but first we want the users to consider if it is really what they want. So, we have identified three viewpoints. One person might look backwards and see if everything is consistent with the statement of requirements; another might consider how easy it would be to produce a system specification from this document; the third might take the viewpoint of a user, possibly with little computer knowledge, who has to understand how the system will work from a business point of view.

For the review to be conducted fairly, the author must know what the document is going to be compared against and have access to it. As well as source documents, standards and guidelines for producing the document and the checklists used to review it should be freely available. Comparison with source documents becomes more difficult if more than one source is used but the principle still holds.

So, here is a general purpose checklist which can be used in most reviews. They look for basic quality criteria such as consistency and traceability. Some of the questions will be found frequently in the checklists provided with the life cycle chapters where they have been made more specific. When you think about what questions are needed for your particular circumstances, it is worth looking at this list to see if there is something relevant.

General purpose checklist

The questions which you can ask of almost any document are:

- Is it complete? Does it contain enough information for any of its likely readers who may not have the same background knowledge as the author.

- Is it correct? Are there any errors of fact?

- Is it consistent? Is there any contradiction between any statements within the document or between this document and its source documents?

- Is it relevant, with every statement having a bearing on the argument of the document?

- Is it precise and unambiguous? Ambiguity can be particularly difficult to discover simply because, when we read a statement, we tend to interpret it in one way and do not imagine it any other way. In a review, the inspectors should be on the lookout for ambiguity. As for imprecision, words such as large, small, much, many, often, quite, fairly should be treated with caution. "The system will process a large number of invoices just before the month end" is not very helpful. "The system will process between 25,000 and 30,000 invoices each day during the five days immediately before the day of the accounting month end" tells you more.

- Is it traceable? Can we trace every statement back to the source documents with nothing extra added here? Similarly, is everything in the source documents which should be dealt with here, actually present ?

- Does it follow the standards, guidelines, checklists, terms of reference or any other criteria used to produce or assess this document?

- Can each statement be verified in some way? This could be by a test, such as a program test, or by reference to another document.

- Is each statement appropriate to the type of document? Beware the statement of requirements which talks about databases, access paths and the like. This is appropriate for a system specification but not for something which should be expressed in business terms.

- Is it readable? This is somewhat subjective but look for well-structured sentences, unpretentious vocabulary. Some authorities try to impose a ban on the passive and to insist on a maximum number of words in a sentence. This is excessive and can actually lead to some very tortuous prose. If you read a sentence and understand it clearly the first time, it is good enough. Occasionally you meet a vocabulary snob who will search the thesaurus for an obscure word as a kind of intellectual one-upmanship. The inspector considering this aspect of the document should not be cowed by this but remember that the readers will not want to consult their dictionaries too often when reading it.

  When a document is actually a diagram, look for clarity above all together with adherence to the rules for drawing the particular type of diagram. This is much easier than for a natural language since there is virtually no scope for subjectivity and personal opinions.

These general points should be considered during reviews together with checklists which have been designed for specific documents. Advice on drawing up your own checklists is given in Appendix 5 – creating your own quality checklists.

During the review each defect will be classified, normally by codes. So, you have one code for ambiguity, another for error of interpretation, another for inconsistency and so on. Each of the categories described in the general purpose checklist above is a defect. In Fagan inspections, they are also classified as missing, wrong or extra and uncertain meaning and then rated by severity. Severity is simply major or minor, the difference being that if major errors are not put right, documents which follow will be wrong.

Quality assurance specialists can analyse the defects and make recommendations for improving quality. If they discover that there are a large number of deviations from technical standards they can investigate further. Are the standards badly written? Is training needed? Are the standards no longer relevant? In this way, the benefits of review go beyond the document currently being scrutinised.

Categories of defect can generally be found quite easily for the questions in the checklists for reviews in the life cycle chapters. In the review of the system proposal (*see* Chapter 3 – Definition), one question asked in the review is;

  Are the levels of service (including such matters as system recovery and response) feasible both technically and from the point of view of costs?

In this case it is not too difficult. If the author has recommended something which is not feasible it could be classified as an error of fact. If the subject has not been dealt with and the author was supposed to do so, it is an omission. Some rework is obviously needed.

Some of questions are not only concerned with defects. Looking on in the same checklist we find;

  In view of the contents of the system proposal, will any other systems be affected in any way not envisaged during initiation?

If the author does not mention whether or not other systems will be affected, can it be taken that he has made an omission? The answer is "yes" – if he or she was told to consider this. But the question is as much a prompt for the project manager who needs to think about the implications for the other systems and for the current project. In general, though, there will be little difficulty in using the review checklists as input for quality assurance statistics as well as assisting in analysing the implications of the document.

REVIEWING METHODOLOGY DOCUMENTS

The possibility of using the life cycle in conjunction with a methodology has already been raised. One of the advantages of a good methodology is that it uses the same methods and diagrams during different phases of the development process. For example a data flow diagram can be used as an aid to describing the current state of a system. The same technique will next be used in order to show options for the proposed new system. When one of these has been selected it can be taken further to become a detailed model of the new system. When it comes to reviewing these diagrams, a number of identical questions can always be asked as a means of judging correctness.

Of course, these questions are not enough by themselves. As well as general questions, specific questions need to be asked about the use of a diagram or a catalogue in context. We need to consider the role of the document and ask ourselves if it is really providing clear, comprehensive answers to the problem it is meant to solve.

This book is not a guide to methodologies and, in any case, there are already numerous works on the subject. A few are listed in the bibliography. Instead it draws attention to methodology documents which can be used within this life cycle as an integral part of the documents described here. Thus a data flow diagram of a system which is being replaced could supplement a statement of requirements by drawing attention to a problem area in the system. Even if you did not want to include a data flow diagram permanently in the statement of requirements itself, it would be a very helpful working document in that it would focus attention on the business activity which is under consideration.

Below is a brief description of three frequently used SSADM diagrams, together with some general-purpose checklists which can be used when reviewing them. Most can be adapted with ease to similar methodologies such as LBMS.

Data flow diagram

Data flow diagrams (DFDs) depict processes; they show how data comes into a system and what happens to it. Once in the system data might remain static in one place or be processed and modified. DFDs also show what events initiate processing, what the limits of the system are and how it is related to other systems (*see* Figure 1.6). A DFD is a very useful method of communicating with others, especially with users since they do not need to be computer experts (or even methodology experts) to understand it, and it is a good way of representing business processes.

DFDs are at their most useful in the early phases of the system but they also have a place in the user documentation, especially a high-level DFD showing how the system works in business terms. A variation on the DFD, known as the context diagram, can show at a glance how the system fits in with others. This illustrates data flows for a small section of a system using SSADM notation. When the customer asks for a spare part, the salesman

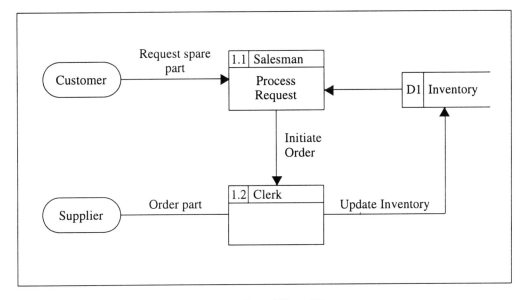

Figure 1.6   Data Flow Diagram

checks to see if it is in stock and, if not, asks the clerk to order it. The clerk orders it from the supplier and updates the inventory to show that the part is on order.

This diagram shows part of this process only. For example, more detail would be needed to show how salesmen initiated the order. Perhaps there should be a form or else a computer generated order be created when the inventory record was updated. A review of a data flow diagram will ask such questions during the early stage of system development.

As working documents, DFDs draw attention to processes which are of questionable usefulness for example where one process duplicates some or all of another process. Such anomalies are often revealed because DFDs are hierarchical, with lower level DFDs expanding on the higher levels. They are also quite comprehensive if taken with other documents. These are elementary process descriptions (EPDs), which describe the lowest level of processing; input/output descriptions, which show what data passes to and from the system; external entity descriptions, which show responsibilities for activity.

The following general-purpose checklist can be applied to any data flow diagram.

- Does each function have a simple, accurate relevant name, preferably containing a verb?

- Does each data store have a descriptive, simple name?

- Does the notation comply with the standards for the methodology?

- Are only permitted connections used?

- If one of a series of upper and lower level DFDs, is it consistent with the others? Consider data stores, processes and external entities as well as data flows.

- Is it clear where the boundary of the system is?

- Are all external entities clearly shown?

- Compared with source documents, does this DFD accurately reflect the system it is meant to represent?

- Are all names unique?

- Are all the data stores actually used?

- Is it clear what the direction of each data flow is?

- Does every data store have a source of data?

- Do the inputs generate outputs?

- Are all the functions you would expect actually given?

Logical data structure

A logical data model (LDM) represents the data, showing the relationship between different groups of data and providing details of every data element in a system. The main diagram is the logical data structure (LDS), with additional detail being provided by entity and relationship descriptions. The two main concepts are the entity, which is a logical grouping of data, and relationships, which is the link between entities (*see* Figure 1.7).

- Does the notation comply with the standards for the methodology?

- Does it match other representations of the data e.g. do entities match data stores on DFDs)?

- Are the entities and relationships correct?

- Is it complete, with every entity and relationship traced back to a source document?

- Are any relationships redundant?

- Has each entity a unique identifier?

- Are the relationships shown actually correct, i.e. mandatory/optional and exclusive/ multiple relationships?

- Are all relationships shown as one-to-many?

- Are relationships given sensible descriptions, preferably with a verb?

Figure 1.7 shows a logical data structure for a small section of the system we saw in Figure 1.6. It shows relationships, for example the notation indicates that a clerk can be responsible for many orders (one to many) and that the existence of orders depends on the clerk.

This sort of diagram is useful in designing data structures and the means of accessing them. This diagram prompts the question: what should the relationship between the spare parts and the inventory records be? We should need more information to answer that fully but it is likely that we should want to access the inventory records at least by part number and order number.

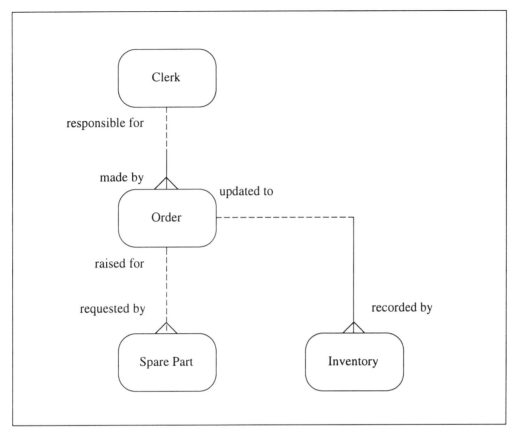

Figure 1.7   Logical Data Structure

Entity Life History

Entity life histories (ELHs) takes a chronological view of the system. They map out the sequence of events and shows their effect on the system and the changes they bring to it. In computer terms, an elh can be thought of as representing the creation of new data, its modification and, finally, its deletion (Figure 1.8).

- Does the notation comply with the standards for the methodology?
- Can the entity be traced back to a source document?
- Can the events be traced to data flows on matching data flow diagrams?
- Can the entity be traced to entitles on a matching logical data structure?
- Does the sequence of events shown in the diagram mirror the true sequence?
- Is the diagram complete in that it includes all events during an entity's life and distinguishes between,
    - events which are mutually exclusive;
    - different occurrences of the same entity type which are treated in different ways?

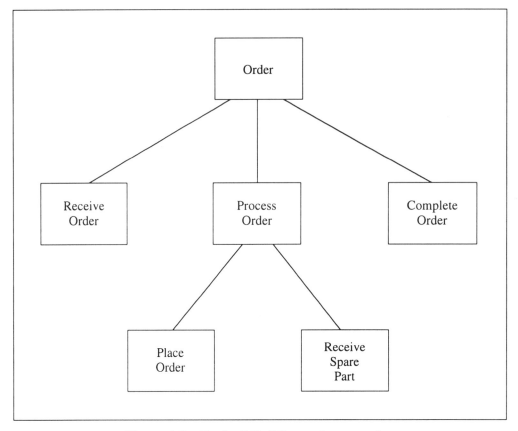

Figure 1.8   Entity Life History for an order

- Do all the events shown really represent change to a data store?

Figure 1.8 is an entity life history for an order. If it is compared with Figures 1.6 and 1.7, it soon becomes apparent that they do not deal with the actual receipt of the spare part at all.

In reality, with more complete diagrams, you would hope for a high degree of consistency. Nevertheless, omissions and contradictions soon become apparent when different types of diagrams are compared during a review.

The three SSADM diagrams shown here are widely used, quite simple to follow with a reading knowledge of SSADM and a little practice. High-level diagrams are suitable for communicating with users. Users of methodologies can supplement these with other diagrams, catalogues and documents. These are aids to quality in that cross-checking is generally straightforward. Taking high-level documents, changing them and enhancing them from phase to phase makes for continuity. This can make reviews easier.

It is not difficult to create your own checklists for other methodology documents. Appendix 5 uses a user role/function matrix as an example.

The life cycle chapters refer to methodology documents which are useful during different phases. You can supplement the checklists given above with questions which apply specifically to the current phase. Some of the documents described in the life cycle may not be single documents at all. A system specification could be made up almost entirely of methodology documents. There is the additional bonus that methodology tables, lists and diagrams used in one phase can be developed during later ones. Some make extensive use of methodology documents as working documents and combine them with natural language in the final version.

However, even when fully committed to a methodology, project teams will be unable to dispense with natural language entirely, even during those phases where the methodology is most useful. A security requirements review or an applications package evaluation will both need some communication in natural language, although diagrams may be useful supporting documents.

Summary

Having considered the workings of the quality life cycle and the principles of review, we shall now examine each phase in detail. With the general purpose checklist (given above under "What should the review look for?"), a review of any document will be beneficial. You can achieve a greater degree of thoroughness by looking closely at the contents of the life cycle documents and asking questions which both consider the detail and which focus on broader contextual issues. Some of these documents may be unfamiliar to systems development practitioners but all are explained in detail before we look at review.

2 Initiation

Of all phases of the life cycle, the first is most important. Yet it is all too easy to produce an unsatisfactory system simply by failing to take sufficient care in finding out what is needed. Computer professionals are quick to dream up computer systems but do not always look closely enough at the business function it should serve. Even their users sometimes think in terms of a familiar system, perhaps one that is being replaced, rather than thinking about what their real needs are. Therefore, careful investigation and effective communication now will prevent disappointment and excessive rework later.

The Initiation Phase is concerned with research. It begins with a problem or a need for which a computer system may provide a solution. It may seem quite straightforward, for example new reports based on existing data may be all that are required. But unseen problems can lurk behind even a seemingly simple request. As far as the users are concerned, there should be no reason why data which turns up elsewhere in one of their systems should not be present in the new one. If you see a figure on your report, why can you not use it elsewhere? A closer investigation might reveal perhaps that it is not actually the users' data at all, or that it is a derived figure and does not actually exist permanently in the form the user imagines. In other words, satisfying a seemingly simple request might involve more work than you would expect.

Sometimes the computer department will receive a written request. This may be phrased in the jargon of the user's profession or, worse still, in a badly understood version of computerese. Even clearly written requests may be open to interpretation. Therefore, however obvious the problem seems, it is essential to look at it closely. The systems manager should ensure that the user's needs are restated in business terms before looking for a computerised solution.

The same will apply even if the initiative for change comes from the computer department. Perhaps it has been decided to use a new range of computers. Sometimes a system has been amended to death, creaking along in a state of near collapse. Merely to limit the exercise to the creation of a carbon copy of the old system is a wasted opportunity. A reappraisal of the user's needs will result in a better system. This is especially true of a much amended system. After all, why does it need so much amendment? Do we want to end up with something else which also needs to be changed frequently?

The statement of requirements will generally be supplemented by other documents. Feasibility studies and cost/benefit analyses are familiar and business impact analyses are becoming increasingly so. It may be helpful to summarise these investigations into a system justification, recommending whether or not to proceed.

The phase therefore has two main review points (*see* Figure 2.1). The first is after the statement of requirements has been written: it considers whether it contains a sufficiently

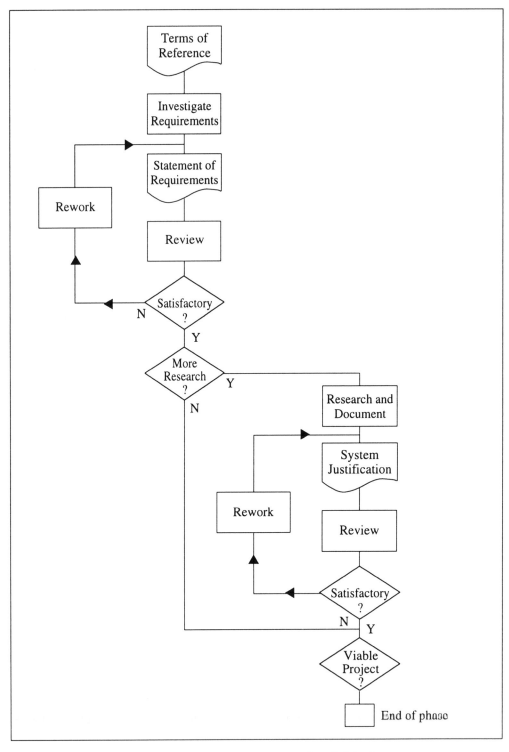

Figure 2.1   Review points during Initiation

clear description of what is needed and whether or not it represents a viable project. Occasionally, the systems manager may judge that this is all that is needed, for example when making minor changes to an old system. Generally, though, further research will be needed, not least because most companies insist on some kind of scrutiny of costs and benefits. The resulting documents will be reviewed individually and summed up in the system justification. The second main review decides whether to proceed with the project.

During subsequent phases of the project, most work involves the use of at least one source document which has been reviewed. In contrast, the requirements may have to be discovered without the benefit of any source document or they may be based on several. Some of these may describe a current system or procedures in the user department, in other words they are not written primarily to state what the needs are. Sometimes there will be no more documents at all and the requirements will have to be defined by interviews.

Rework and revision are particularly important during this phase. Interaction should be the norm (*see* Figure 2.2). After the statement of requirements has been written, it may be modified by subsequent research. Perhaps users have not given serious consideration to security, believing it is someone else's problem. Participation in a business impact review may open their eyes. Flexibility and a willingness to review and modify documents in the light of subsequent research will ensure that this phase results in a clear understanding of what is required for the project.

Phase initiation

The phase normally begins with one of the following:

- the user raises a problem or points to a need which might be solved by the use of computers;
- the user requests a new version of an old system;
- the user reads or hears about a computer system and thinks it might be useful;
- the user requests amendments or additions to an existing system;
- the computer department decides that an old system needs to be replaced.

In all cases, any computer system must be seen to fulfil a business goal. The systems manager will want to make sure that this is what is at least implicit in the request before proceeding with it.

Control of the Initiation Phase

At this stage, we are ascertaining what the requirements are and whether or not they form the basis of a viable project. Detailed planning for the rest of the project is not necessary until a decision to proceed has been made, although some estimates of the scale of the project will be needed.

In many cases, especially for enhancements to existing systems, this process will be simple enough. Difficulty arises if producing a clear set of requirements proves difficult or if subsequent investigation becomes protracted. It is all to easy for discussions about the user's needs to drag on and on. The systems manager can reduce the risk of this happening by drawing up terms of reference which provide a framework for the phase.

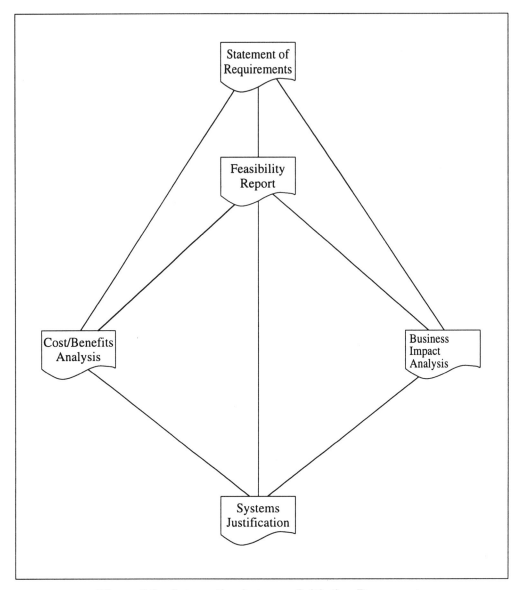

Figure 2.2   Interaction between Initiation Documents

These clarify the limitations of the investigations, name people who should be consulted and give sources of information and timescales.

Contents of the terms of reference

The following points should be considered when drawing up the terms of reference for any of the documents produced during this phase.

- What is the reason for the investigation?

- Who is responsible for the investigation?

- When must the investigation be complete?

- What sources of information are available? The person responsible for the investigation may discover sources unaided but should be given as much assistance as possible. Useful sources might include:

  - a written request from the user;

  - internal memoranda, manuals and other documents from the user department;

  - the documentation of a current system;

  - articles in journals describing a similar system;

  - literature describing a software product, for example an accounts package.

  If an old system is not properly documented, the terms of reference should ask for a concise overview of the old system and its data. A context diagram or high-level data flow diagram and logical data structure will be useful working documents.

- Who should be interviewed? Interested parties who should be considered include:

  - a user making a request;

  - colleagues who obtain information from a current system and who might be affected;

  - those who actually use a system which is going to be replaced for their day-to-day work and computer staff who support it;

  - external users, f or example other companies supplied with data;

  - customers .

- Which users can provide helpful information about the area under investigation? For example, they may assist in providing background information about their business area.

- What are the limitations of the investigation? Examples are:

  - time limits;

  - budget;

  - software and hardware.

- What documents must be produced by the investigation and by when?

  When the investigation of the requirements begins, it may not be clear how much further research is required. The terms can be written to allow for possible extensions or modified later. For example, the systems manager may decide that the solution is likely to be an applications package. The author of the feasibility study would then be directed to consider this option.

- Are there any special requirements regarding the investigation or the contents of the documents? The systems manager may be aware of circumstances which need to be taken into account. For example, some parts of the reports may have to be confidential.

It is important to provide access to as many interested parties and relevant sources of information as possible (*see* Figure 2.3). In this way, the investigation will be more likely to avoid focusing too narrowly on a stated problem and be able to find out what lies behind it.

Documents

The systems manager may decide that a statement of requirements should be written before considering if other documents are needed. However, a feasibility study and cost/benefits analysis should be mandatory if a new system is being written, if a major enhancement is needed or if a choice has to be made between a number of possible solutions. For example, it may be that the computer department is deciding whether to

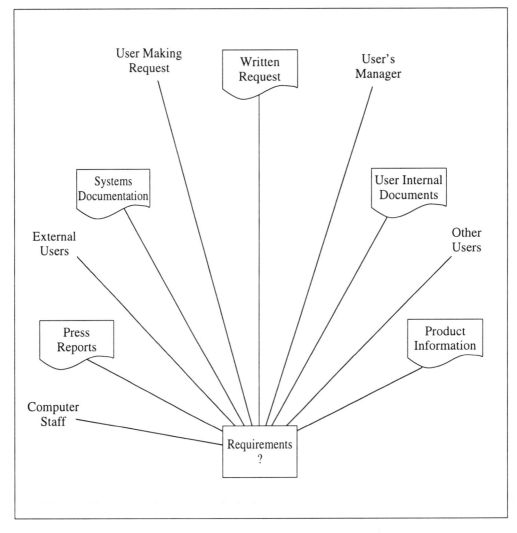

Figure 2.3   Sources of the Requirements

continue using mainframes or changing to networked PCs and wants to weigh up the advantages and disadvantages of both. Investigation into feasibility, a comparison of costs and benefits and examination of security will enable a considered choice to be made. Equally, the benefits of a user request for access to an expensive external database might be compared with those obtained from providing the same service internally. In most cases an 'in-house' computerised solution will at least be considered as an option in the feasibility study.

The systems manager might also decide that further investigation is needed for amendments if they:

- require new data structures or alter new ones;
- interface with other systems;
- access external systems (i.e. not under control of the same company);
- are complex;
- might be met, at least in part, by an applications package;
- might be the subject of a prototype;
- have security implications which suggest that current practice may be inadequate.

To sum up, the documents produced during this phase are as follows.

- Statement of requirements
  - Target audience: users;

    project staff;

    computer centre management.

    This is a key document.

- Feasibility report
  - Target audience: users;

    project staff.

- Cost/benefit analysis
  - Target audience: users;

    project staff.

- Business impact analysis
  - Target audience: users;

    company security management;

    project staff.

- System justification
  - Target audience: users;

    project staff;

    computer centre management.

Statement of Requirements

This is one of the most important project documents since it is the principal source of all others in the life cycle. It is also difficult to ensure it is correct because, unlike many subsequent documents, it will probably not have a single source which can be readily reviewed. Its aim is to state as simply and clearly as possible what the problem or need is and it does this in business terms. No solution should be offered. Only when it has been accepted, i.e. signed off by the user as an accurate statement of what is needed, can the project commence.

Sometimes the number of sources and the variety of their quality make the task of assessing the requirements a difficult task. Appendix 3 'Reading difficult documents' is intended to make the assessment of written texts easier and will be more helpful here than during any other phase of the life cycle.

Although the statement has to be written in business terms and should be free from computer jargon, care should be taken to make sure it is going to be understood not only by users but by systems development staff working on the system who may not be completely *au fait* with the terminology current in the business area. It is also advantageous for the author of the document to make sure that he or she has understood properly. Therefore, any business terminology should be explained if it is not obvious or something which can be found in a normal dictionary. A computer person might be expected to know (or to find out with little difficulty) what 'profit and loss statement' meant. Unqualified reference to an 'unencumbered allotment' is more likely to cause problems.

The statement should be detailed enough to identify the roles of different types of users and what they do. It may be tempting to take this for granted and assume that it can be sorted out later. But different roles imply different processes and access rights so the statement should identify them on security grounds if nothing else.

Performance of processing, security and system interfaces should all be considered now. Perhaps the requirements will include calculations which are currently performed by staff using tables (such as insurance or tax tables) and a calculator. Since they are known, why not include them in the statement, at least as an appendix? Alternatively, a reference to a source which contains the calculations, such as a government publication, should be included.

The fact that the requirements are expressed in business terms should not be taken as meaning they should not be precise. Perhaps the users want a new system so they can look up information quickly. The statement of requirements should say how quickly. How long should it take to find the information? I may think that a minute is long enough: a user with a customer on the other end of a phone would regard this as hopeless. Even if the user is vague at first, a discussion of scenarios in which a new system is used should enable you to introduce a greater degree of precision. We need a figure, a time expressed as a number of seconds. The review of the statement of requirements will look for vagueness and ambiguity.

A few diagrams or tables will help the reader. This is especially true of a replacement system. Some of the users may not be conversant with computer methodologies but most people can easily understand a context diagram or high level data flow diagram. A user catalogue will show the roles users played in both old and new systems. These diagrams are very helpful if you need to contrast how a system works currently and how it might work in future.

As for the contents, consider the following points when preparing the statement.

- What are the reasons for the requirements?

  Frequently, they will refer to problems or limitations encountered in using an existing system, which may or may not be computerised. Other common reasons are opportunities for savings, improved service to customers, efficient working or greater competitiveness. Sometimes, the reason may be entirely external such as a change in the law. At all events, the system should have an explicit business goal.

  If a replacement is being considered, contrast what is happening now with what the user wants to happen when the system is written.

- What perception of the system does each user have? As Figure 2.4 shows, different users can have very different ideas about its function based on their own experience. If a system is going to be replaced, is there any risk of losing any benefits? These may not have been considered by the person requesting a new system.

  Above all, beware of making assumptions about the needs of particular users, even if based on the views of people who think they know. The opinions of the latter may be no more than a stereotype of what they think the user is and what he or she should need. Do you conform to a stereotype?

- Is the new system one which is going to be audited at some time?

- If the system under consideration is a replacement, is the current one used properly? It may be that some useful features are overlooked.

- Have users changed their expectations of their current system? Perhaps it was a first computer system for them and was introduced when the sole point of comparison was a manual system. It is also possible that it contains features which were the brainchild of someone who left the company long ago and of no interest to anyone now.

- What are the main features of the proposed system in business terms? It is acceptable to refer to the performance of an existing system or to point out that the system may have technical implications, such as those given below, but no elements of systems design should be present.

  The use of diagrams and tables should be considered here.

- Might there be any implications for other systems or other users? For example, the source of data may be a computer system controlled by another department in the same company or by another company. Although agreement to provide data may have already been given, this may have been without realising that extra work will be needed.

- Are any new or special skills likely to be needed within the computer department? It is worth considering this especially if the computer department has no previous experience of a business area. For example, a department may use complex statistics which only a highly-trained mathematician could understand. This might have implications both in terms of staff skills and software requirements.

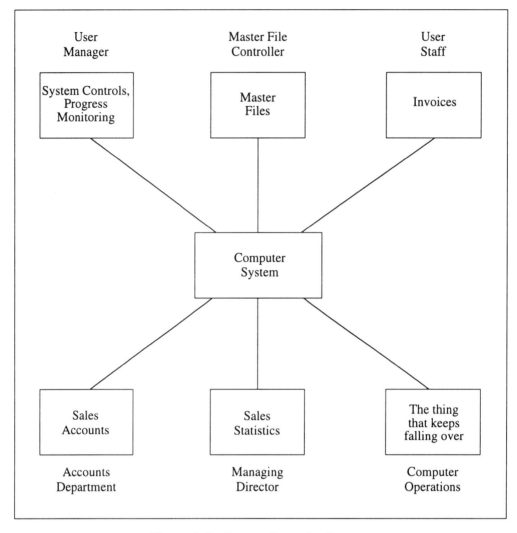

Figure 2.4   Perceptions of a System

- What volumes of transactions are anticipated? Are any peaks likely, such as month or year end processing for financial systems? This might impinge on other systems as well or it might mean that processing capacity and performance need special consideration.

- Do any of the requirements appear to have legal implications? For example, if the data refers to live human beings it may be necessary to take account of data protection legislation of countries where the system will be used.

- Are there any security issues which need further investigation? Even simple data extraction might need further investigation. How confidential is the data? How valuable is it? Where is it going, Who will see it? If there are any doubts about it or fears that current security practice may fall short, security needs assessing.

- Are any time limitations being proposed? These will have to be met if they are imposed by legislation.
- Has the possibility of subsequent modification of the requirements been raised? If a database may later be used as the source of an executive information system, this will have implications for the systems design.
- Are there any technical or financial constraints on the system? If there are budgetary limitations, will it be possible to offset development costs against potential savings from the system?
- Is any requirement at odds with the terms of reference for this statement?
- Will the system depend on further information being provided by the user? If so, when will it be available? It should be ready during the Definition Phase.
- In addition to the possible problem areas given above, are there any limitations or areas of concern?
- Are the sources provided in the terms of reference adequate? It is worthwhile mentioning who was interviewed and what documents were used. If, for example, a manager decides his staff should not be consulted even though they use the current system, it is worthwhile seeing that this fact finds its way into the report.
- How long will the system be required?
- How long will the data be required? Data held in archives should be considered.

Feasibility Report

A feasibility report should be written in order to decide whether or not a computerised solution is possible. 'Possible' does not only mean technically feasible; the proposed system must also be acceptable to the user and be within time and cost limits. Normally, details of the costs and benefits would be dealt with in a separate report. However, the feasibility report may well list several possible solutions but be able to dismiss some on costs grounds simply because the costs will obviously be way beyond budget.

The starting point of the feasibility study is the statement of requirements. It must be possible to trace back all possible solutions to this. The feasibility report may be drafted in conjunction with a cost/benefits analysis and business impact analysis. Thus, the possible expense of elaborate security benefits may make a computerised solution infeasible, given the constraints imposed on the development of the proposed system. Similarly, a detailed analysis of the costs of two feasible solutions may eliminate one. An interactive approach is needed.

The aim is not only to show which solutions are feasible but to highlight one as optimal so that the feasibility report can be used for making a clear, positive recommendation. Of course, if none is feasible, the report should show this. While it is preferable to prove that one solution is better than the others, there may be little to choose between some of them. A cost/benefit analysis will help here.

A packaged solution?

The systems manager may decide that it would be easier not to write some or all of the proposed system. Many applications are available as packaged software. Although a package will probably not meet all requirements, for example integration with other systems, it may well provide an easy solution to the majority. Therefore, the project may be mainly an evaluation of one or more packages.

Once the requirements are fairly clear, the systems manager may consider whether packages should be investigated and direct the author of the feasibility study to do so. The feasibility study can compare application packages just as it would compare various option of 'in-house' development.

The systems manager's decision will be based on experience. In addition, the following should be considered.

- Are there a number of possible candidates on the market which might provide a solution to the requirements? This is most likely if the system is a well-defined business area which will be found in most companies. For other areas the choice may be limited or non-existent.

- Will the proposed system interface with others?

- Are the requirements for the system likely to change? Although a package supplier will normally respond to legal changes, other changes might only come about after considerable customer pressure and at cost. Individual customisation may be very costly.

- Will it be possible to develop the system 'in-house' in time?

These factors should be considered when deciding whether the feasibility study should encompass applications packages.

Contents of the feasibility study

The following points should be taken into account.

- What, briefly, are the main features of the proposed system? The statement of requirements should be mentioned here.

- What, in outline, are the options which are being put forward in this report?

- For each of the options, provide the following information.

    - What are its main functions?

    - How well does it meet the requirements?

    - To what extent does it not meet any of the requirements?

    - Is new hardware or software required?

    - What additional training or experience would be needed?

    - How would staff be affected?

    - What would be the approximate cost of development, operational expenditure and other financial implications? Where there is more than one reasonable solution, this will probably be expanded in a costs/benefit analysis, although there is no point in performing such an analysis if the option is shown to be infeasible in this report.

- How does it measure up against any constraints set down in the statement of requirements?

- How does this option compare with the others? If one is obviously the best solution, state why. A matrix comparing features will be useful here.

Diagrams will highlight the contrast between the different options. High level data flow diagram and data models are a useful way of presenting the options simply and accurately.

If computer packages are being considered, the checklists given in Appendix 1 under 'Questions for the supplier/ manufacturer' should first be used when dealing with companies providing packages. Particular attention should be given to two questions.

• Can the package be integrated with other systems and processes, including security arrangements?

• Is the data readily accessible for extraction by other processes?

Other factors will be important (*see* 'Questions for the supplier/ manufacturer') but these two are essential if the package is going to be integrated in any way and if the data might be used for other than the processing contained within the package.

Costs/benefits analysis

To produce a useful, accurate costs/benefits analysis can be time-consuming. As few optional solutions as possible should be analysed.

The source document will be the feasibility report, if one exists, or else the statement of requirements. If the project manager has decided to omit a feasibility study since only one solution is under consideration, a description of the proposed solution will be needed of the same level of detail as would be given to an option in a feasibility report.

The aim of the analysis is to examine the requirements and solutions in order to answer the following questions.

- Is the project worth pursuing?

- Which approach is best if two or more are under consideration?

- Is one way of producing the system better than others? A packaged solution might be considered as an alternative to 'in-house' development.

Where quantifiable data is available it should be used. However, benefits may be intangible and they should not be overlooked simply because a figure cannot readily be put on them. A company may want to invest in a new computer system because it will improve management decisions. Although it may be possible to give an example of how the system might do this, trying to show the results in terms of income will probably be fruitless. Simply to list such intangible benefits is not enough; 'improved management decisions' is too vague by itself. Show how the system would work so that managers could use it to improve their decision-making.

Costs/ benefits analyses have to be prepared with company rules and procedures for doing so in mind. Some companies insist on great detail while others are content with a fairly general assessment. Also, if work is being done for another company, it might insist on more detail. The examples shown here are not complex but include ways of comparing benefits and on assessing intangible benefits.

Project costs are most likely to be reasonably accurate if they are based on comparisons with completed projects of approximately the same size and complexity. It is also easier to obtain good operational costs if the hardware and software is the same as for other systems. If we are considering a new operational environment, it might be possible to find answers from another company which uses it. Where a packaged solution is under consideration, purchase and maintenance costs should be available from sales literature.

The costs and benefits will mainly be obtained from the user department or computer department. It is important to persuade those providing them to be accurate and realistic. It may be necessary to ask for the basis of estimates. All benefits should be explained. Above all, it may be necessary to probe more deeply and show that someone's pet scheme is actually flawed and has serious disadvantages.

The following are the most important costs, benefits and comparisons which should be considered.

- estimated project costs;
- estimated operational costs;
- cost comparison between alternative solutions;
- comparison with current operational costs;
- tangible benefits;
- intangible benefits;
- comparison of the benefits of alternative solutions;
- comparison of benefits with those of the current system.

Also, a recommendation of the best solution should be made.

There is no need to include all of these in every costs/benefits analysis. There is no point including a section on intangible benefits if the sole aim of the system is to save money The author should show why any sections chosen are relevant. Only if the answer to the following three questions is 'yes' should the section be included.

- Is there good reason for including this, i.e., is it something which has a bearing on why the project should go ahead or on the comparative advantages or disadvantages of one possible solution?
- In view of the data available, can a reasonably accurate estimate be arrived at?
- Is this sort of cost or benefit worth considering for the sort of system under consideration?

It is important to point out disadvantages, even of a solution which is obviously better than others. A disadvantage may well be a potential source of problems for the future and, if this is the case, it is best to look for ways of dealing with it at an early stage.

Here are some questions which should be asked during the analysis.

Estimated project costs

- What are the direct costs of developing the system? These may include:
    - new hardware for this system only, including development hardware;

- new software for this system only, including development software;
- travel and accommodation expenses;
- applications packages (whether used in conjunction with 'in-house' development or as an alternative);
- stationery, forms, etc;
- training;
- contract staff, consultants and other external personnel.

- What are the indirect costs of developing the system? Typical are:

  - computer department staff costs;
  - user department staff costs;
  - shared hardware costs, including development hardware;
  - shared software costs, including development software;
  - computer resources used in the project.

Obviously, staff costs will depend on numbers, salaries and the length of the project. These can only be very broad at this stage but it should at least be possible to compare costs for different options fairly. There is generally no benefit in allocating part of departmental budgets for heating, lighting, etc. These costs will be incurred whether or not the system is written. Some companies might wish to do so and, obviously, company rules about such matters have to be considered.

Of the costs given above, salary information may be difficult to obtain, especially for users. There are also pitfalls in including it in reports since individual salaries might be shown or made easy to discover. A project may be cross-charged to a user department although a company may feel it is not necessary to show 'in-house' staff costs on the grounds that staff will have to be paid any way, in which case only contract staff will have to be considered. An estimate of overtime working is not likely to be of much use at this stage. Estimates should be based on actual costs but, during this phase, can only be approximate.

Estimated operational costs

- How many users will be required to operate the system effectively? This should be expressed by job category and man hours.

- How many staff in the computer department will be needed to operate the system?

- What will be the staff costs for both users and computer staff? The figures for current staff and new recruits should be shown separately.

- What are the costs of:

  - computer equipment (including networking, storage, backup equipment);
  - maintenance charges;
  - replacement costs;

- power;

- office equipment, etc?

If new staff will be recruited and new equipment purchased in order to run the system, the costs should be shown separately. It is more difficult to apportion costs for current staff and shared equipment and such information is sometimes of questionable relevance for costs/benefits analysis. If the system under development merely uses a small amount of surplus capacity on a mainframe computer, is it worth your while trying to put a cost on it? Similarly costs for current staff are not significant if they will continue to draw their salaries whether the system is written or not.

Cost comparison between alternative solutions

If alternative solutions are being analysed, a comparison of the costs for each should be given, with any substantial differences highlighted. While a suitable table or matrix will make for ease of reading, it is worthwhile providing explanatory notes if there is any risk of misinterpretation.

Comparison with current operational costs

If a system is being investigated in order to replace another, a similar comparison should be made between the actual running costs of the old system and those estimated for each of the solutions under investigation.

Tangible benefits

Tangible benefits are quantitative and are expressed as sums of money. They include all savings and increased income which it will be possible to attribute to the new system. Again, if there is more than one feasible solution, values should be shown for each.

In most cases, details of these benefits should be obtained by asking the user, especially if increased income is one of the reasons for investing in a new system. The user should also put a figure on savings which might be made. For example, if the system means that external services or agencies will no longer be required since everything will be done within the department, a reasonably accurate estimate of the savings can be made. Sometimes discounts are available if operations are completed within a certain time, such as the payment of fees for maintaining intellectual property registrations. Any such savings should be included.

Savings and increased income may be linked. If a new system enables staff to work more quickly and accurately, it should be possible to give them extra duties or to take on more work. This can in turn be shown in terms of increased income and reduced unit costs.

Reduced operational costs, whether for users or computer staff, should also be shown as a benefit.

Intangible benefits

How do you put a figure on an intangible benefit? One commonly used method is to apply factors to the benefits, for example on a scale from 1 to 10. If one of the intangible benefits is ease of use, the author of the report may decide that one option under consideration will merit 8, another 5 and so on. This looks good on paper, especially when comparing the relative merits of different options. It also focuses the mind of the reader on the relative benefits of different solutions. Of course, such a method is subjective and somewhat arbitrary even when a comparison is being made between products which exist. If we are writing a consumer report on washing machines, at least we can actually try them out before awarding points. Here we are dealing with solutions which only exist on paper and the result must be more subjective.

It is possible to make the process more sophisticated by applying weightings. Take Figure 2.5 for example. Here some intangible benefits are shown and, on the face of it, option 1 is better since the total score for all three is higher than that given for option 2. Is this reasonable? Perhaps so, if all three intangible benefits are of equal importance. But we have to ask – is this really likely? The answer is that probably one benefit will outweigh the others.

Let us say that improved speed of processing is the main reason for wanting a new system, followed by ease of use and finally by less need for data preparation. Having discussed these benefits with the users and other interested parties, it should be possible to apply factors to each of the intangible benefits. Figure 2.6 shows the same intangible benefits and the same scores. The difference is that total scores for each option have been modified by the factors. Now option 2 is clearly to be preferred as far as intangible benefits are concerned.

Sometimes it is possible to make a broad guess at potential earnings or savings resulting from an intangible benefit. If it is believed that the system will lead to better management decisions, this could be expressed by showing that more income will result.

All intangible benefits should be explained, showing examples of how the system will actually produce them. Better management decisions may result from access to a database holding worldwide marketing information because it will allow your company to pinpoint where it should be selling its product and deciding its pricing policy.

Many people in business find comfort in figures and prefer to see things expressed in this way. However, they will rightly ask questions about the basis for such figures and care should be taken to show that there is some foundation for your optimism.

	Option 1	Option 2
Speed of processing	2	8
Ease of use	5	2
Less need for data preparation	8	4
	15	14

Figure 2.5.   Comparative intangible benefits – without weightings

	Option 1	Option 2	Weightings
Speed of processing	2	8	10
Ease of use	5	2	5
Less need for data preparation	8	4	2
	61	108	

Figure 2.6.   Comparative intangible benefits – with weightings

These are some examples of intangible benefits:

- improved management decisions;
- increased competitiveness;
- flexibility in staff deployment;
- flexibility in systems use, e.g. scope for user reporting, data extraction etc;
- ease of use;
- expandability;
- improved quantity and quality of information;
- improved speed processing, perhaps eliminating a bottleneck currently causing problems;
- improved communication;
- replacement of an inefficient, out-of-date system;
- less need for data preparation, possibly eliminating bureaux services;
- greater systems reliability;
- reduction in contact with the computer department in order to keep the system running.

Comparison of the benefits of alternative solutions

A matrix is useful here as a way of making the comparison. The main problem is doing so for intangible benefits but the simple use of factors and weightings explained above makes for clarity. Some explanation of why one benefit is considered more important than others should always be given. Whether or not matrices are used, obvious advantages or disadvantages should be drawn to the readers' attention.

Comparison of benefits with those of the current system

This is very useful if a system is being replaced. The same remarks regarding presentation given above apply here.

It should not be forgotten that sometimes an old system will have advantages which will be lost. The user may be enthusiastic about the benefits but encouraged also to state what problems might ensue. Examples are:

- staff no longer have enough work and face redeployment or redundancy;

- work is no longer skilled and staff may become bored and demotivated;

- the system may mean that staff have to spend more time using the computer and less time on other activities which may be neglected;

- staff may tend to rely on the computer and lose knowledge and expertise which is crucial for other aspects of their work;

- when all information is stored in the computer, provision of a service may be jeopardised if the system fails unless security measures are introduced.

Recommendation

Unless it is obvious that the system is not worth taking further, the report should conclude with a statement saying which is the best option.

Business impact analysis

At any stage during the Initiation Phase, the systems manager may decide that security needs special attention. Typically, something will emerge during the preparation of the statement of requirements which suggests that current security arrangements may not be adequate. Therefore, it will be necessary to investigate the potential impact of a security breach and to review the project in its light.

The following are examples of cases where a business impact analysis should be seriously considered:

- the user expresses concerns about security;

- one of the requirements is for an exceptionally high level of security;

- the requirements imply a need for a very high level of security for which current practice may not be adequate;

- the requirement s suggest that the data for the system or the processing may be very sensitive or very important .

During this phase, risk can best be considered in terms of business impact. Although users may not consider security, unless prompted to do so and the statement of requirements does not deal with risks *per se*, security implications should be considered when the statement of requirements is reviewed. The best method of making the user think about security is to discuss scenarios. What would be the implications for the company if this happened? Ideally, this should emerge during discussions with the user department on the statement of requirements.

The scenarios should be presented solely in terms of business impact and solutions should not be considered. It is important to prepare some suitable scenarios before discussing them. These will provide evidence of the need to consider risk, and act as a stimulus for further discussion. It is very useful to dream up 'worst possible' scenarios and to ask the user to consider the possible consequences. Starting from this gloomy prospect, move on to think about the real likelihood of such a disaster happening.

Many people think of only two kinds of computer security problem, namely hacking and computer viruses. They do so with good reason for both have been well publicised but others should also be considered. Three categories are used to describe all breaches of computer security, namely confidentiality, integrity and availability. It will help to focus attention during a business impact analysis if these categories are used.

The terms used and the scenarios envisaged in this exercise should deliberately be focused on the implications for a business. Obviously, suitable scenarios will vary from company to company and from system to system. The examples given below are only for guidance.

Confidentiality

What could the impact on the business be if information held on this system or produced by it was accessed by an unauthorised person?

What might happen if the information was divulged? Could it lead to:

- loss of competitive advantage;
- loss of public confidence;
- loss of business;
- extra expenditure;
- legal or contractual liability?

There follow a number of examples which are applicable to one or more of each of these categories. This may be of use but you will probably have to think of some of your own.

Loss of competitive advantage

- Marketing plans are revealed to another firm. From these the firm can work out what our marketing strategy is and take steps to undermine it.

- Our firm has invented a new product. Before we have been able to apply for patent protection, a rival has obtained details, claims patent rights for itself and then makes a fortune out of our product.

- A pricing plan has been accessed and is now in the hands of a rival. It shows where we are going to make reductions and increases. The rival can now use this to undercut us.

- Another firm is planning to take over a firm in our area of business activity and our firm appears very suitable. It has obtained details of our plans for the next five years which will be very useful for its takeover strategy.

- Our firm has done a lot of work, deciding which trademark names will be suitable for a particular area, having considered the legislation of several countries and current registrations in those countries. Another firm has discovered our strategy and can now give its lawyers material with which to delay or deny our registrations.

Loss of public confidence

- A leak to the press reveals full details of a new product before the company wanted to announce it.
- Confidential reports are released to the press which show that a new product is not as effective as claimed or may have unpleasant side effects. The fact that these reports may be inaccurate, out-of-date or taken out of context is irrelevant – it smacks of a cover-up.

Loss of business

- A rival intercepts our orders and uses the information to undercut us.
- A rival has access to detailed records of sales and can work out who our best customers are. The next step is to use this information to target these customers and try to win them over.

Extra expenditure

- We give discounts to a long standing customer. Another customer discovers this and insists on being treated in the same way. Of course, if not satisfied, this company could take its business elsewhere and make sure other customers know why.

Legal or contractual liability

- Confidential agreements with other firms are made public, including agreements for licensing new products and other forms of cooperation.
- Details of staff salaries are made public by a discontented member of staff who makes sure that all can see last year's pay increases for managers.
- A headhunting agency accesses details of the salary, conditions and experience of key staff.
- A terrorist group discovers the personal details, including home address, of staff involved on a key research project.
- Shortly before the company results are officially announced, they are published in the press.

Integrity

What might the impact on the business be if information held on or produced by this system became inaccurate, was lost or was supplemented by unauthorised data?

Data can be corrupted by accident or by design. Fraud, where someone commits fraud using a computer, is a well-known example. However, data might be deliberately corrupted for other reasons, for example records might be altered in order to cause embarrassment. There is also the possibility of accidental corruption such as data duplication.

What might happen if data was corrupted? Could it lead to:

- loss of public confidence;

- potential fraud;

- loss of business;

- extra expense;

- bad management decisions;

- legal or contractual liability?

At this stage, it is useful to think of realistic scenarios, which might point to the inclusion of controls when the system is written.

Loss of public confidence

- Customers are sent the wrong orders or do not receive anything.

- The company publishes information about its performance but this turns out to be based on inaccurate information on the computer.

Potential fraud

- Duplicate invoices are added to the system.

- Records for non-existent clients are added to a system.

- A customer claims that only part of an order has been sent. Our computer shows that the amount ordered and the payment received was for the amount dispatched. The customer's copy of the order supports his case: our bank statement supports ours.

Loss of business

- Customer name and address records are altered. Some disappear, others are altered so that names and addresses no longer match.

- Credit ratings are reversed so that persistent debtors are shown as good payers and vice versa.

- Orders are wiped off the system or the amount and type of order changed.

Extra expense

- A manual system using temporary staff has to be brought in, in order to sort out inaccurate data and keep the business running.

- Goods are not sent on time because the orders have been mixed up. Therefore, we must pay compensation.

Bad management decisions

- The company's five year plan is based on inaccurate information.
- A valuation of the company's assets is based on erroneous data and, consequently, they are underinsured.

Legal or contractual liability

- Personal information is shown to be inaccurate in contravention of data protection legislation.
- Financial reporting is based on incorrect data and misleading information about the company's tax position has been recorded.

Availability

What might the business impact be if the system's data became unavailable or became very hard to access because of poor performance?

A system might become unavailable because of loss of power, faulty hardware or software or even a major disaster such as a fire in the computer room. Slow response, for whatever reason, can lead to work piling up and might even persuade some that it is better not to bother with the computer.

In either case, the main categories of potential damage are:

- loss of competitive advantage;
- loss of business;
- loss of public confidence;
- a backlog of work;
- bad management decisions;
- extra expense;
- legal or contractual liability.

The scenarios given here include examples both for total loss of availability and poor response.

Loss of competitive advantage

- Details of all companies interested in a new product cannot be accessed, allowing a rival company with a similar product the opportunity of getting in first.

Loss of business

- New orders cannot be entered into the computer and current orders cannot be followed up.
- Reminders for late-paying customers cannot be dispatched.

Loss of public confidence

- Payment demands are sent to customers who have already paid because the payments were not processed in time.
- We have to announce that orders will be sent out late because of technical problems.
- A new product is not launched on time because the publicity depends on data held in the computer.

A backlog of work

- Large amounts of data are added to the system every day. When the computer fails, manual records are used. When the system is restored, there is no time to add both the manual records and new data.
- Data from this system feeds into others, which depend on it as a source of current information used to validate other data. When the system fails, the others cannot be updated and their business activity suffers as well.
- Staff cannot keep up with the normal pace of work because response is so poor. Consequently, one month's processing is still taking place while data for the next is piling up.

Bad management decisions

- Sales statistics are not available and decisions have to be made on out-of-date data.
- An agreement with another firm must be signed soon or the other firm will look elsewhere. Our information about its market share, which we need to make our decision, cannot be accessed.

Extra expense

- Temporary staff have to be employed and overtime worked in order to keep a system operating manually.
- We cannot meet our contractual agreement to provide information to another company in time and have to pay compensation.

Legal or contractual liability

- Staff cannot be paid since the payroll system cannot be accessed.
- Statutory reporting of accounts cannot be completed in time.

Assessing the risks

Clearly, there is little point in considering hypothetical situations unless some attempt is made to measure their seriousness. Although an estimate of potential loss in monetary terms may be sought, it is easier to use a points system showing a scale of seriousness. During this phase, the aim is to identify areas of concern so that they are included in the requirements for the system.

It is easy enough to draw up forms using the three main categories of risk and, within them, the types of impact given above (see the appendices for examples). Discussion of scenarios with users should decide what points should be given.

A scale from 0 to 4 such as the one given below is easy to use. Availability is slightly more complicated because the length of time for which a system is unavailable has to be taken into account. Periods of one hour, one day, one week and one month should provide enough focus. As for slow processing, it can help if you think in terms of missing one hour, one day or one week per month.

- 0 No business impact whatsoever;

- 1 Minor impact only;

- 2 Significant impact;

- 3 Very serious damage;

- 4 The company's survival could be at stake.

If these can be translated into concrete examples, so much the better. Imagine the scenario centred around the leaking of information about a new product. This would probably rank as 'very serious' in terms of potential loss of competitive advantage and would receive a ranking of 3. It would be better if it could be expressed in a report as, say, "up to three years competitive advantage could be lost". A further improvement would be to refine it still further with a statement such as, "£30,000,000 of income could be lost to another firm".

Reporting the Business Impact Analysis

This analysis requires close scrutiny of the scoring notes of the scenarios discussed. The following checklist should be used.

- Do all the zero scores appear to be reasonable? Remember, this means that security is not a problem. If there are any doubts, they should be re-examined. The fact that zero scores are recorded does not mean that they should be overlooked in the report.

- If there are any ratings of four, do they appear reasonable? Any such ratings should be reconsidered and, if it is thought that they are sound, brought to the attention of the company's security department or whoever is responsible for disaster planning.

- What can be learned from the other ratings? Any pattern or trends should be highlighted. For example, it might become apparent that confidentiality is a minor consideration but that every thing points to the importance of keeping the system up and running. A graphical representation of the results will help here.

- Did the user mention any security requirement during the course of the discussions? If so, it should be mentioned here.

- Does the experience of the computer department suggest that systems of this sort need special security requirements?

- If a replacement for an existing system is being considered, does experience show that the current system is vulnerable?

- Are we aware of any specific threats?

- Could there be any legal implications?

- Are there any obvious safeguards which might be mentioned? If, for example, it is stated that division of responsibility is needed, controls can later be built into the system.

- Are there any obvious implications for costs or time spent in developing the system?

- Is there anything which should be used to modify the statement of requirements? Discussion of risk scenarios may lead to the user giving serious thought to this. The report should recommend this. A single sentence will normally suffice, for example:

    "If the system becomes unavailable for any reason, it must be restored within a single day in order to prevent significant loss of business."

- What other recommendations does the author have regarding the development of the system or for the company's security practices?

System justification

A system justification recommends whether or not to proceed with the system and states why. It is useful to write one for large developments where a statement of requirements has been supplemented by much other research. The research documents may have been much amended and contain information which is no longer required. The systems justification is aimed partly at management, both user and computer, who will have the last word as to how the system will be developed.

Less technical and detailed than the research documents, a good system justification summarises the research and makes a well-supported recommendation. If reviewed against all its source documents before release, it will provide a sound basis for continuing the project.

In writing the system justification, the following should be considered.

- What are the main features of the proposed system? It is sensible to make reference to the statement of requirements.

- What are the main points to emerge from the research? These should be classified under feasibility, costs and benefits and business impact.

- Which findings support the decision to recommend proceeding or abandoning the project?

- If recommending that the system should be written, does the research point to any *caveats*? It might be possible to go ahead but at considerable cost.

- Is it proposed to go ahead with some of the requirements but not all? If so, state why some are going to be omitted.

- What are the main features of the proposed system? A high level data flow diagram and a data model will be useful here.

- What are the implications for other systems?

- What might the implications be for other development work if this project goes ahead as planned? It might be necessary to delay other work or make changes.

- How big a project will this be in terms of staff?

- How long will the project take to complete?

- Have any future changes or enhancements been identified?

- How long is it anticipated that the system will last?

Is a prototype needed?

What if the users are not completely certain about the sort of system they need ? The value of the feasibility study will be diminished if it cannot remove this uncertainty. The requirements may be clear enough but the preferred solution may not.

A good prototype removes doubt and uncertainty by enabling the user to respond quickly to new features of the system. It is suitable for online systems and should be regarded as the normal way of developing expert systems.

Prototyping should be considered during Initiation and the system justification is the best place to consider it. It should be discussed with the users and their agreement to the method is necessary, not least because it requires a high degree of user involvement.

The section of the system justification dealing with prototyping should consider the following.

- What is the aim of the prototype? It should not be used to find out what the business requirements are although they may change when the users have seen the prototype. Typical goals are:

  - rapid development;

  - evaluation of optional solutions;

  - improved communication with users;

  - clarification of areas of uncertainty as to how the system will function;

  - specification of some or part of the system, for example the standard screen and menu handling routines;

  - a chance for users to evaluate all or part of the complete system through a model.

- Which of the requirements can be turned into a prototype? Sometimes a subset of a difficult or important area will suffice. Examples of prototypes are:

  - an expert system;

  - a model of a complete system with reduced functionality;

  - part of system of which the functionality is representative of the whole;

  - a part of the system which requires interactive processing;

  - a system which provides a large number of variable processing options.

- Are there staff available with experience of prototyping work? If not, what are the implications for training?

- What user resources are required? Are the users aware of the commitment and involvement required of them?

- How, broadly speaking, will the project timescales be affected? A comparison with timescales for conventional development should be given.

- What would determine that prototyping was complete? A document detailing the aims of the prototype and the extent to which the prototype has achieved these aims should be considered.

- What would determine the success or failure of the prototype?

Review

As was stated above, there are two main review points in this phase. The first is the review of the statement of requirements and the second is the review of the system justification. Both are important because so much depends on them. The user must accept the statement of requirements before the system can proceed and management of both the user department and the computer department must agree that the system justification shows how to proceed.

Consider a full, formal software inspection, of the sort advocated by Michael Fagan, for both of these documents before submitting them to the user for agreement.

Review of statement of requirements

- Does the statement adhere to the terms of reference?

- Do the detailed requirements match the original aim of the investigation?

- Is it a statement of requirements *per se* or does it attempt to provide a solution, especially one in terms of systems development?

- Does it contain anything which cannot be traced to other documents, for example, systems documentation or user correspondence, or anything which appears to be at odds with them? If so, does it state why?

- Does it contain anything which suggests further research is needed? Reasons include:

  - security implications;

  - potentially high costs;

  - choice of possible solutions;

  - implications for other systems;

  - implications for other business areas;

  - resourcing difficulties (including new skills, staff numbers, effect on other projects).

- Does it provide information which is clear and adequate enough to translate into a computer system? It should describe how things will be done and who will do them – processes, functions, data and users.

- Is anything expressed vaguely? If anything is imprecise, is a good reason given and when will this be clarified?

- Is it written in such a way that its meaning can be readily understood by users and computer staff?

This document may be reviewed again if it is amended after costs, risks and feasibility have been considered, especially if no system justification is written. However, it should never be more than a statement of requirements, unless the systems manager has decided to incorporate some extra material here and has asked for it in the terms of reference. See above under 'Documents'.

Feasibility report

- Do the contents conform to the recommended contents for this document ?

- Is it completely consistent with the statement of requirements with nothing altered, added or missing?

- Are the alternatives truly feasible ways of meeting the requirements?

- Does it analyse the advantages and disadvantages of each, including:
    - time constraints;
    - ease of use;
    - staffing levels;
    - training;
    - user preference;
    - control requirements and other security features;
    - hardware/software?

- Do comparisons always use the same criteria consistently?

- Does the report consider packaged software? If so does it address the following questions?
    - Has it identified suitable candidates?
    - Will they perform all the requirements we want them to? If not, how easy will it be to make up for these deficiencies?
    - When compared with 'in-house' development, does each package provide a solution which is at least as good?
    - Do the candidates appear to provide data . accessible by 'in-house' procedures?
    - Is integration with other systems feasible?
    - Are our security standards met by the package's own security requirements?

    – Have the questions for the Supplier/Manufacturer (*see* Appendix 1) been used in selecting candidates? Have they indicated anything which makes the recommendation of the feasibility report questionable?

- Is there sufficient detail for this document to be used as a source for costs/benefits analysis?

- Has anything emerged during discussions about feasibility which has become a requirement? If so, the statement of requirements should be modified.

Costs/benefits analysis

- Do the contents conform to the recommended contents for this document?

- Is it completely consistent with the statement of requirements with nothing altered, added or missing?

- Does it deal with all alternatives given in the feasibility report, except those which were ruled out?

- Are the bases for the estimates reasonable?

- Are the benefits genuine and do they represent valid business improvements? Examples are:

    – cost savings;

    – efficient operation;

    – better data;

    – efficient access of data and improved reporting;

    – greater security;

    – cost control;

    – improved planning?

- Are intangible benefits included? Are they realistic?

- Has anything emerged which should be included in the statement of requirements?

Business impact analysis

- Do the contents conform to the recommended contents for this document?

- Is it completely consistent with the statement of requirements with nothing altered, added or missing?

- Are all the scenarios reasonable and possible?

- Do any of the scores appear to be outlandish?

- Does it limit itself to problems or does it attempt to provide specific solutions e.g. a product?

- Is it complete in that every type of scenario applicable to this system has been considered?

- Is there anything in the statement of requirements which implies risk? If so, is it dealt with here?

- Is every significant finding converted into a requirement which can be included in the statement of user requirements?

- Has anything been identified which should be part of the statement of requirements but which has not been included?

- Does the document imply anything for our baseline security practices but which has not been stated?

System justification

- Do the contents conform to the recommended contents for this document?

- Is it completely consistent with the statement of requirements and other source documents with nothing altered, added or missing?

- Are the arguments justified by reference to other documents produced during this phase?

- Are the assumptions made in recommending a solution really valid?

- Is there a positive recommendation about how to proceed, supported by valid evidence?

- If it is recommended that the project should go ahead, does it appear suitable for a packaged solution? If not, will it be necessary or desirable to use the services of a bureau?

- Has prototyping been recommended? If so, the following questions should be considered.

  - Is the aim of the prototype a reasonable one? In particular, is it discrete and manageable?

  - Does the area selected for the prototype appear suitable (e.g. interactive processing)?

  - Is it compatible with the aim of the prototype?

  - Are the timescales compatible with those for the project as a whole?

  - Can the staffing requirements, including user involvement, training, etc., be met?

  - Is the user representative empowered to make decisions about the suitability of the prototype as the basis for subsequent development?

  - Will the prototyping exercise end with something, for example, a report which can be reviewed?

End of phase

The Initiation Phase ends when the systems manager is satisfied with the statement of requirements and, together with the other documents, there is sufficient information to recommend proceeding or not with the project.

If the statement of requirements has not been agreed by the user in its revised form, this should be obtained before proceeding. User agreement to points raised in the system justification should also be given.

The major decisions about the project will be made on the basis of the system justification. Unless it is decided to farm the work out to a bureau, we know now what the system will do and, broadly, how it will do it. We also know the way in which the system will be developed, straightforward 'in-house' development, using an applications package, or by building a prototype. The next phase, Definition, begins the project in earnest.

3 Definition

The project takes shape during the definition phase. The rest of the project is planned now and a project manager appointed to oversee all activity connected with the system until it has been accepted as a live system after implementation. If this activity is well planned, there is every hope that the system will be a success. As a first step the project manager should draw up a plan encompassing both the total project and, in more detail, the current phase. Long term planning is more important and the project manager has to decide which of his team will be responsible for which activity, determine criteria for judging the success of these activities, arrange meetings and other channels of communication with the users and others with an interest in the project and conduct regular reviews.

It can be difficult to devise a project plan which is acceptable to everyone but which you feel confident is truly feasible. Pressures such as deadlines have to be weighed against the need to produce a system which works well. When a project is large, when it uses unfamiliar software or development methods, it is all too easy for the project to fall flat on its face. The project manager can assess the risks of that happening and show what needs to be done to ensure success. If a project is understaffed in view of its complexity and the timescales allowed for it, is it really viable? Can the shortfall of staff be made up?

Important decisions now have to be taken about how the system will be developed. In a straightforward 'in-house' development, the statement of requirements is converted into a system proposal which describes a computerised solution. It is the basis of all the subsequent development work and is a key document which should be kept up to date throughout the life of the system. However, there are other options. Did the system justification show that an applications package could provide a solution? If so, a major part of the project will be the evaluation and implementation of a package. Packages sometimes provide a complete solution by themselves but often they will have to be modified or used in conjunction with 'in-house' development. Some points about package evaluation and checklists are given in Appendix 1. During this phase, we are concerned with deciding for which functions a package can be used and getting the evaluation off the ground.

The users have agreed their requirements, now they have to agree the functionality of their system. It goes without saying that communication with them is of great importance and that all documents should be written with this in mind. But, what if the users cannot make up their mind about the functioning of the system? It might be a case for a prototype. A prototype may have been recommended during the initiation phase. Even if it has not, it is still not too late to decide to use a prototype to find the best way of performing some functions (*see* the checklists in Chapter 2). Prototyping is a useful technique so long as it is well controlled. If not, it can develop into a 'permanent prototype', which grows and grows and eventually becomes an unsatisfactory substitute for a well-designed system. During definition, a prototype should be planned. Thus, determining the functionality of the system may go ahead on three fronts.

Setting quality objectives is now a normal part of systems development. Although quality practices are an integral part of this life cycle and the project plan should provide for review of documents, it may be useful to draw up a separate quality plan during this phase. It is particularly beneficial if the computer department is fortunate enough to have a separate quality assurance section. Such a section will provide assistance in selecting and conducting reviews and inspections, in training and in measuring the project team's success in attaining the quality objectives. Lessons may be learnt during this project which will benefit future work.

Even if security has been considered during the initiation phase, it may still become an issue now. It is possible that something will be discovered while working on the system proposal which makes closer scrutiny of security important. It is still not too late to carry out a business impact analysis, although this may mean altering the statement of requirements in consequence. Also, the project manager may decide to include a security requirements review in the project plan as the best way of converting security requirements into solutions .

In short, the project manager has to make a number of key decisions which will determine the future of the project and not merely consider day-to-day supervision (Figure 3.1).

Phase initiation

Definition begins when the statement of requirements has been written and the system justification has shown that a feasible computerised solution exists. Normally, user consent to both should have been obtained as well. What if this is delayed? Should valuable time be lost because company rules dictate that a director must give consent to a project and that director is on the other side of the world? Obviously practice will depend on the company's rules and politics but it is unlikely that anyone will thank the systems manager if he refuses to allow anything to be done on an urgent project because of a formality. The systems manager may judge that some preliminary work should begin before obtaining formal written consent under the following circumstances.

* The system is straightforward, viable and will not incur extraordinary costs.

* The systems manager knows from experience that agreement is likely. Sometimes a proposal has to receive formal approval from a director and this might take a few days. If the user for whom the system is being written can assure you that this is a mere formality, why wait?

* Some of the staff who will make up the project team are available.

* The system is going to be developed under externally imposed constraints such as tight deadlines.

There is obviously a certain risk in beginning work because the user may turn round and demand changes or even decide to scrap the project. Therefore, such work should be limited to drafting a project plan, thinking of how to convert the requirements into a system, considering what might be suitable for a prototype or making preliminary inquiries about packages.

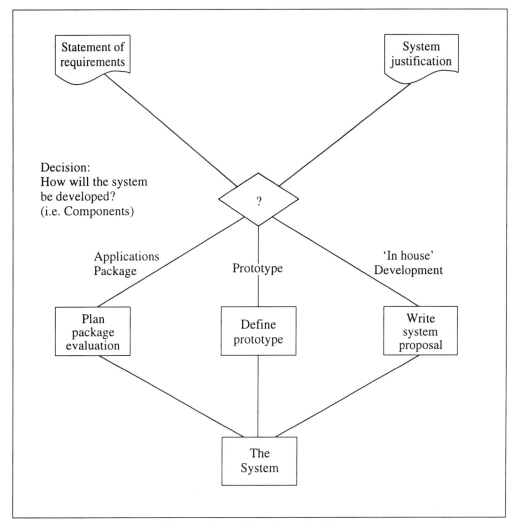

Figure 3.1   Planning decisions

Documents

Two documents only have to be written during this phase, namely the project plan and the system proposal. Both should be carefully reviewed as much depends on them. The project manager will review the project plan throughout the life of the project, revising it where necessary. Care at this stage will minimise the need for change later on.

The system proposal is a key document which will be maintained for the life of the system. Some of its contents will be part of an applications package which will be planned now. If prototyping seems a viable option, it will be defined during this phase.

Apart from these, the project manager may decide to draw up a separate quality plan and review any special security requirements.

In summary, then, these are the documents which may be produced and reviewed during this phase.

Main documents

- Project plan
  - Target audience: all those working on the project.
- System proposal
  - Target audience: users;

    project staff;

    computer centre management.

This is a key document.

Optional documents

- Quality plan
  - Target audience: project staff;

    quality assurance staff.
- Prototype definition
  - Target audience: users;

    project staff;

    computer centre management.

This document will normally be written after the system proposal has been reviewed if prototyping is to be used. It becomes part of the project plan.

- Package evaluation plan
  - Target audience: evaluation staff;

    project staff;

    computer centre management.
- Security requirements review
  - Target audience: users;

    computer security staff;

    project staff;

    computer centre management.

Once again, the keys to success are flexibility and an understanding that you will probably only obtain the final versions of some documents after others have been reviewed (*see* Figure 3.2).

In addition, new requirements might emerge or new concerns about security may make a business impact analysis advisable during this phase. Both would involve revision to documents produced during Initiation and user consent (*see* Figure 3.3).

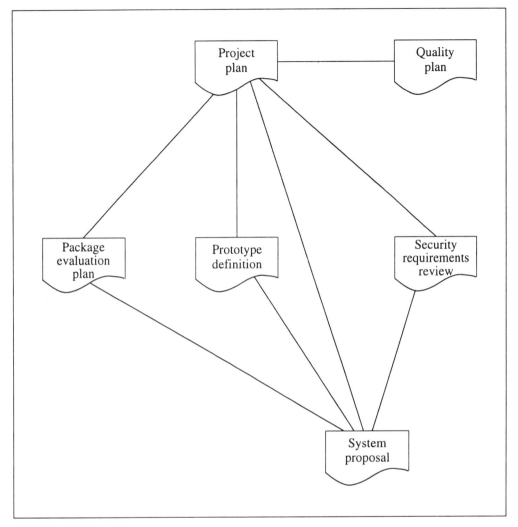

Figure 3.2   Interfaces between Definition documents

Project plan

Of all the life cycle documents, the project plan is the one most subject to revision. It remains in use until the project is complete. During this phase, three main areas have to be considered:

- the management of the project as a whole until completion;
- the management of the current phase;
- risk assessment – a consideration of the viability of the project .

The project plan should be reviewed whenever work on a new phase is about to commence and should be amended whenever necessary. When a new phase begins, the project manager should draw up a detailed section for the current phase using the overall

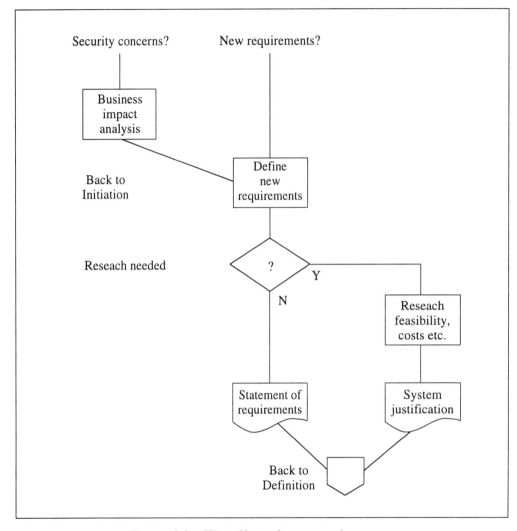

Figure 3.3   The effect of new requirements

plan as a basis. It is also an opportunity to remind those taking part in a particular phase of their commitment to do so. It is advisable to record this information now.

The assessment of the viability of the project involves looking at risk. For many projects, particularly small ones in familiar areas of systems development, this will not be needed. Even if the project manager does not consider risk during the first draft of the project plan, its review may indicate that a project risk assessment is desirable.

Day to day administration of the project, such as setting deadlines and allocating work, may be simplified by using project management software. It can be very useful when controlling a large project, since it should eliminate elementary miscalculations and show possible areas of conflict, for example, where the same member of staff is shown as working on two different activities simultaneously. However, the project manager should to be guided by experience and his or her own ideas on how to run a project and not subject to the *diktat* of a machine. Therefore, the project management software should allow for human intervention, frequent changes, the inclusion of extra activities, rework and so on.

In addition, project management software should be able to cope with 'what if?' questions, especially for long-term project planning. It should not be necessary for the project manager to laboriously enter precise details of estimated hours worked by each individual when planning work months or even years ahead on a project just to make the project management software function properly.

The following checklists should be considered when drawing up the plan. Project managers may not be responsible for some items, such as those relating to finance. They are included here for completeness.

The project as a whole

Here we are looking at the long term and there is no point in being over-precise during this phase. Greater precision will be possible as the project develops. Although estimating is difficult, the experience of similar projects can be taken as a yardstick. It is wise to allow for some contingency, especially when untried technology is going to be used for the first time, when a business area is unfamiliar or when the type of system is completely new. Otherwise the project manager may be under considerable pressure to skimp the latter phases of the project because of a commitment to a self-imposed deadline. Users will generally prefer to look forward with confidence to their system being implemented between, say, the end of May and the end of June next year, if they know that a more precise date within that period will be forthcoming later.

This part of the plan is a framework for the project, including rules for communication, change control and so on.

- How long will it take to write and implement the project ?

- When will the system be implemented?

- For this phase and each of the subsequent phases of the project:

  - what are the activities;

  - how long will each of these activities take;

  _ what will be produced (including documents);

  - what will be reviewed;

  - how will it be reviewed (i.e. the method to be used)?

- What is the estimated duration of each phase?

- When will each phase begin and end?

- How long will the system run before the post-implementation review?

- What is the estimated total length of the project?

- are there any time constraints such as those imposed by law or by business needs?

- what are the staff numbers required for each phase? This should be additional information showing what type of staff are needed (e.g. programmers and systems analysts), the level of experience required and staff availability.

- is any new software needed? If so;

  - when will it be needed;

  - when will it be available?

  Distinguish between software for the system and software for project work only, such as analyst workbenches.

- Is any training needed, for example, in new skills or new software? If so, when can it be arranged?

- What user involvement will be needed during each phase? For each phase, consider:

  - who are the users;

  - what will their roles be;

  - will they be managed as part of the project team;

  - when will they be required and for how long:

  - are they aware of their roles in the project;

  - is their availability guaranteed by their managers?

  Distinguish between users available for consultation and those who play an active role in the project.

- Who else will the project team need to communicate with? Consider:

  - suppliers and other external companies;

  - computer staff, especially computer operations.

- What are the rules for communication? Consider who the people are whom project staff need to contact. Sometimes it is best to make one project team member responsible for dealing with an individual or company. It is important to consider arrangements within the computer department, too.

- Are there any special rules about documentation and standards? Do not forget to make sure that contract staff are made aware of what the rules are.

- What are the procedures for controlling changes and version numbers? See Appendix 2 – Managing Change.

- Which tasks depend on the completion of others and which can be worked on simultaneously?

- What is the total budget for the project? From this, deduce in broad terms what proportion of it should be spent on each phase.

- Is prototyping going to be used? This will normally be added after the system proposal has been reviewed and agreement reached as to the extent and the purpose of the prototype. This is dealt with below under 'Prototype Definition'.

- Will any part of the system use packaged software? This will be finalised after the system proposal has been written. See below under 'Package evaluation plan'.

Everyone who will be working on the project should be sent a reminder of his or her involvement, together with anticipated dates. Precise timing for later phases may not be possible, hence the need to deal with each phase in turn when it is due to commence.

The current phase

Since this part of the project plan is more concerned with day-to-day management, a greater degree of precision is needed here. Even so, some contingency is advisable. Timings can go awry if, for example, the extent of work on the security requirements was not appreciated at first.

- What are the activities which have to be done during this phase?
- What will each produce?
- How long will each take to complete?
- What determines completion, for example, document ready for review?
- Who are the project staff working on each activity?
- When will they be available and how much time can each spend?
- When will reviews be held?
- What form will the reviews take?
- Who will take part in reviews?
- What involvement of users and other non-project staff will be needed during this phase? Consider:
  - who they are;
  - what their roles are;
  - when will they be available;
  - how much time can they devote to the project?
- What is the budget for this phase? How precisely will it be spent?

It is worthwhile reminding those working on a phase, and their managers, of their involvement both now and shortly before the phase begins.

Risk assessment

How will the project manager decide the extent to which the project needs to be monitored to make sure that it will produce the system intended? There is no point in creating unnecessary work. The project manager's own experience will provide guidance in many cases, especially when dealing with familiar sorts of system and familiar hardware and soft ware.

Sometimes, though, it is helpful to take a more methodical look at risk. It is particularly useful to do so in the following cases.

- The project is very large, employing scores or even hundreds of development staff.
- The project requires new and unfamiliar technology, working methods or is concerned with a totally new systems area.

- The project is very complex, perhaps interfacing with several other systems, using a variety of different software. Equally, the complexity may result from the need to provide something which will satisfy a large number of very different users, perhaps in different working environments.

- The project is going to upset a lot of people, for example by making them change their working methods. This need not be the result of conservative thinking on the users' part. They may well have well-grounded, sincere fears that they will not be able to do their job properly under the new system. For whatever reason, willing cooperation will not be forthcoming.

- There is pressure for results with unrealistic deadlines and an over-optimistic implementation date. As a result, the temptation to cut corners, for example, by skimping on testing, may be hard to resist.

Some of these scenarios will be familiar to many who work in systems development. There have been well-known cases of projects being completed years late, greatly over budget and which were not properly tested or implemented. A much publicised example in 1992 of a system which was insufficiently tested and poorly implemented was a system installed in London for controlling emergency ambulance calls. It failed and had to be replaced by manual working. Public sector disasters become well-known precisely because they have such a high public profile. It is not unreasonable to assume that other projects fail for similar reasons.

During the initiation phase, the project manager may decide to consider what could go wrong with the project and what the effect would be. Any of the types of problem given above could result in the project being implemented late and well over budget, or even abandoned completely.

Therefore, the project manager should consider the following.

- What aspects of this project could put its successful completion at risk? Is it one or some of these categories?

  - project size?

  - project complexity (technical, interfaces, etc)?

  - unfamiliar technology?

  - project staff problems (e.g. numbers, inexperience)?

  - user-related (e.g. staff morale)?

  - pressures for rapid results?

- Do the potential problems affect part of the system only, for example, a single area which needs special technology?

- Can the problems be solved by the project team alone? If not, who should be consulted?

- What steps can be taken to monitor the problems?

- What steps can be taken to make sure that the problems do not get out of hand?

The project manager can then consider what measures will reduce the risks and amend the project plan accordingly. They might include some of the following.

- Hiring or employing staff with special skills.

- Making sure that staff who will be responsible for implementing new, unfamiliar technology are trained and acquire experience before they use their new skills in the project.

- Allocating the most competent staff to the most complex areas of the system.

- Monitoring progress of work in key areas very closely so that any slippage is noted immediately.

- Making sure that reporting lines are effective, especially if the system is large.

- Assessing the true effect of late implementation. If, for example, it can be shown that the company will lose a lot of business if the system is three months late, it might be a case for more resources.

- Where problems are to do with morale, ensure that the function of the system is explained and that staff have an opportunity to voice their concerns.

The above are only a few examples. The point of this exercise is to make sure the project plan takes account of any potential problem areas.

Quality plan

A quality plan may be considered as an extension of the project plan. It is a useful means of making sure that quality objectives are met and of communicating with quality assurance specialists. Essentially, the quality planning which was contained within the project plan is recorded and expanded here.

The following checklist should be considered.

• When will formal inspections and reviews take place?

• Which documents will be subject to these inspections?

• What review techniques will be used in each case, e.g. Fagan software inspections?

• What methods of measurement will be used?

• What will be recorded for quality assurance statistics, e.g. types of defects?

• Who will analyse and measure the results of the inspections? This should be a QA department if one exists.

The plan should be reviewed at the beginning of each phase.

Prototype definition

If the system justification recommended that prototyping should be a feature of this development, planning should begin during this phase. The overall project plan will include a section on the prototype. When the system proposal is ready, its review will reconsider just how much should be the prototyped and its aims.

It is most important to ensure that the aims of the prototype are properly stated so that nobody will have any doubts as to its limitations or expect that it can be used as a full system if it achieves its aims. In view of the ease with which prototypes can take on a life of their own, the following should be considered.

- What sort of model will the prototype be (i.e. demonstration and evaluation or something to be converted into part of the final system)?

- How many models will be needed, e.g. for comparison?

- What are the aims of the prototype and how will success be judged? This has been considered under system justification but needs to be restated?

- How will the results of the prototyping exercise be shown? Normally a report should be written to demonstrate how the goals have been met.

- What parts of the system are going to be prototyped?

- Is it a scaled-down version of the full system?

- What resources and how much effort will be needed for the prototyping exercise? Include project staff, users, consultants, etc.

- Who will be in charge of the exercise?

- When will the prototype be complete?

- By what date will the evaluation of the prototype be complete?

- How will the rest of the project be affected by the prototype?

- What language or software tools will be used to create the prototype?

- What will be done with the model (including its data) when the prototyping exercise has been completed? Agreement with the users should be reached as to whether all or part of the prototype will be deleted or converted into the new system. Users may not appreciate the difficulty of convert a scaled-down model of the finished system.

The project plan should show the prototype as a separate activity with its own timetable.

Package evaluation plan

The system justification will have indicated whether a package might be a solution to some or all of the requirements. Generally, some requirements only will be met. A payroll is perhaps the best known sort of applications package, but even these need to be integrated into a new environment. Interface, with other systems and management reporting are two areas where work will be needed, however adaptable the package may be.

One difficulty is knowing how much of the new system will be covered by the package and how much will have to be written 'in-house'. A short list of candidates will have been prepared during Initiation and the functions of these systems will indicate which requirements will be dealt with by the packages under consideration and which will be the subject of the system proposal. This may have to be changed as the evaluation progresses since a manufacturer's perceptions of the function of a system may be different from that of its customers. However, any reasonable manufacturer will respond to a carefully worded description of the functions sought and it should be possible to arrive at a reasonably clear dividing line between package functions and 'in-house' functions.

The system proposal will also describe how the package fits as part of the new system. It will also describe interfaces between the package and other systems.

During the Definition phase, then, the evaluation will be planned. The following items should be considered.

- Which packages are going to be considered?

- What are the limitations imposed on the evaluation? These may include:

  - type of hardware, software operating system or network;

  - costs (purchase, maintenance, etc.);

  - time limits.

- When will the evaluation begin and when will it end?

- Who will be in charge of the evaluation?

- Who will the members of the evaluation team be?

- Which users will be involved?

- Which computer staff should be consulted?

- How will the evaluation team communicate with the rest of the project team, for example, weekly meetings, regular progress reports?

- What documents will be produced by the evaluation team?

- What sources of information should be consulted? There may be correspondence, technical literature and, of course, the statement of requirements and other documentation produced during the previous phase. In addition, there are some general points on evaluations in Appendix 1.

- What are the requirements which are going to be looked for in the packages under evaluation? A distinction between essential and desirable functions may be useful here although you should be clear as to what is meant by these terms. Desirable for whom? 'Desirable' might mean no more than "it would be nice for the users if the system did this but they can do without it". It might mean "this feature would save the project team from having to develop this part of the system 'in-house'".

Figure 3.4 shows an easy method of recording each requirement in a kind of table. The evaluation itself belongs to the next phase.

System proposal

The system proposal describes how the proposed computer system will work. It shows how requirements laid down in the statement of requirements will be met and also any others prescribed in the system justification.

The system should be described in broad terms and in language all can understand: detailed systems analysis will not begin until the next phase. There will be three categories of reader. First and foremost are the users, who should learn how their system will work. Therefore, it is necessary to make sure that it is clearly written and that technical terms are

Requirements	Source	Essential/Desirable	Product
Pay staff either weekly, monthly or quarterly.	SOR31 page 3 item 1.	essential	Easypay Superpay Salaries
Permit BACS transfer or print cheques.	SOR31 page 3 item 2	essential	Easypay Superpay
Require manager Authorisation to add new rewards directly.	SOR31 page 3 item 3	essential	Easypay Superpay Paysys

Notes:
'Source' should refer to a document, e.g. Statement of Requirements and section. 'Product' gives all products under review which fulfill the requirement.

Figure 3.4   Simple reworking of requirements

kept to a minimum and always explained. If any diagrams are used, they should be readily understood without special training and supported by written text. Users cannot be expected to grasp the detailed intricacies of the notation used in methodologies. However, high level data models, data flow diagrams and entity life histories should be readily understood and will make for clarity.

Next, there are the project staff. They will use the system proposal as a source document for all subsequent development work. It goes without saying that any lack of clarity may result in a rather different system than was intended.

Finally, there are other staff in the computer department, especially those on the operational side. They have to plan, too, for training, installing new hardware and software, staffing and so on.

The source documents are:

- the statement of requirements;

- the system justification or other Initiation document which states which of more than one optional solution will be chosen;

- a working document containing a description of the new system, including diagrams in the chosen methodology, if the project manager decided to omit the feasibility study and system proposal.

- a security requirements review (if one is carried out).

People to be consulted are (*see* Figure 3.5):

- computer operations (service levels, hardware, storage requirements);
- computer security specialists;
- staff responsible for data management (to check for possible data duplication);
- systems development management (to check for possible functional duplication);
- users (details of calculations, etc.);
- other companies (product details);
- legal department (compliance with legislation);
- users of systems which will be linked to this one;
- staff conducting a package evaluation.

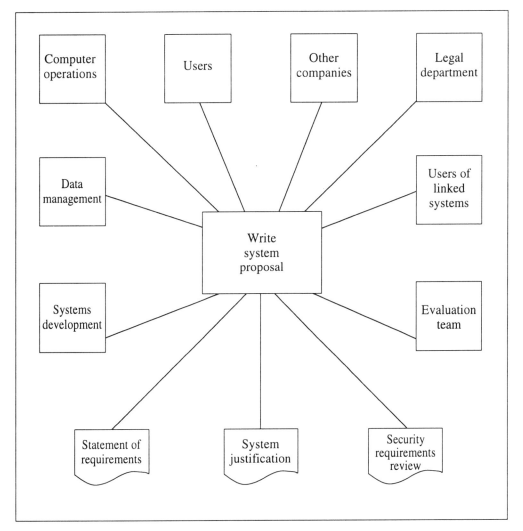

Figure 3.5   People to be consulted

The system proposal may well be revised both during this phase and subsequently when the system is operational. It should therefore be kept up-to-date and re-issued as a complete document whenever changes are made.

It should be accepted in writing by the users as the basis of the system before work begins on other phases.

The layout of the system proposal will vary from system to system. However, it is recommended that it should include a summary of the system in business terms before its functions are described in more technical language. Also, although the system proposal is a high level document, it should be as accurate as possible. If the system performs detailed calculations, these should be fully described. Normally, such calculations are used in the user department and it is a question of setting them out clearly.

Estimates should always be described as such.

The following checklists should be used when considering the contents of the system proposal.

Data

- Where does input data come from?
- How does it get into the system?
- When is it input to the system?
- Does any data come from other systems? If so, how and when?
- What determines that data will be input to the system?
- How do we know if and when data is input to the system?
- What validation is needed for input data?
- Where is the data used?
- What data is transmitted to other systems? What happens to it after transmission?
- What output, including reports, will be produced by the system and when?
- Who receives the output?
- What determines that data is transmitted or output?
- Is *ad hoc* reporting required?
- Is *ad hoc* user access to data required? If so, for what purposes? Examples are reporting, copying to spreadsheets or graphics packages.
- Do the audit requirements suggest that any additional special access may be needed?
- What volumes of data will be processed?

Processing

- What calculations will be performed?
- Which processes modify data and how is it altered?
- Is speed of processing or fast access of data a requirement?

- How does each process affect other parts of the system or other systems?
- What .initiates each process?
- Who is responsible for initiating each process?
- What functions, if any, are going to be carried out by an applications package?

Security

Generally, a computer installation provides a standard level of security for such matters as backup storage, recovery procedures and basic access control. It should not automatically be assumed that it will be adequate for a new system but it can be used as a starting point. In any case, the project manager may decide that a security requirements review is needed (see below) to examine security more rigorously. Security specialists should be involved.

- Are there any special security requirements in the source documents? How can they be translated into features of the system?
- Which users are responsible for granting access rights? How will this be done?
- What categories of systems user have access rights to which parts of the system? What can they do? Include computer operations and users outside of the users' own department.
- What audit facilities are needed?
- What management controls are to be included?
- Are any steps required to ensure compliance with the law, for example data protection legislation?
- What backup and archive requirements are there?

Software, hardware, equipment, etc

A computer installation will generally have a standard range of computer equipment and software. It is most important to highlight anything which is new.

- What new hardware or software requirements are there? This should include peripherals such as document scanners and printers.
- Are any new networks needed?
- Are we familiar with the type of hardware, software, etc, needed for the system? Draw attention to unfamiliar compliers and operating systems.
- Will the system access external systems such as commercial databases?
- Are there any special stationery requirements?

Operational

- What are the anticipated storage requirements?
- What level of response is needed? Note any special requirements?

- What level of system availability for on-line access is required? Is out-of-hours working going to be needed?

- What processing peaks are likely, for example, regular system use, special runs, year end processing? What demands will be placed on computer operations at such times?

- What repeated processing requirements are anticipated? Can a processing timetable be drafted?

- What effect will the new system have on the operation of other systems? Will others be altered in any way or become redundant?

- Which of the requirements identified so far are at odds with current installation standards and practice? Note any features of the system such as service levels, backup and recovery procedures, which differ from those presently in use.

- To what extent will operations staff be involved in the day-to-day running of the system? How will it affect their workload?

- Will there be any likely effect on the numbers of operations staff?

- Will operations staff need to learn any new skills?

Other considerations

- If the user is paying for the system, how much is it likely to cost? Development and equipment costs from the costs/benefits analysis may be included after being checked again.

- Are all the requirements being met? If not, which ones are not being met and why? Distinguish between those being delayed and those being abandoned indefinitely.

- Do any of the requirements conflict with current practice and standards or company rules? If so, state why this is justified.

Security Requirements Review

Security should always be considered when writing the system proposal. In some cases, it may be advisable to treat security requirements separately in a security requirements review and incorporate the findings in the system proposal later. The review should be carried out by someone with security and systems development expertise.

This activity is recommended if security is critical. A computer installation should have certain security standards and a security requirements review should be undertaken if it appears that they will not suffice. A review should also be considered if new technology is being used for the first time.

The main source document is the statement of requirements, particularly those requirements which deal specifically with security or those where security is a consideration. The review ends with a report, describing how the system can be made secure. After review, solutions will be incorporated into the system proposal and reviewed with it.

The exercise may draw attention to some unpalatable facts. For example, the company's security practices may be shown to be inadequate for this system. Does this mean that the practices need to be changed and that current levels of security are inadequate? Is this system a special case? The repercussions may go beyond the current project (*see* Figure 3.6).

Some of the investigation parallels work on the system proposal. Security is a feature of most computer systems and the checklists provided for the system proposal allow for this. The project manager will have to set terms of reference for the system proposal and this report to avoid duplication of effort. Needless to say, cooperation between the author of the system proposal and the author of this report should be encouraged.

The following checklists should be used in deciding what countermeasures are needed.

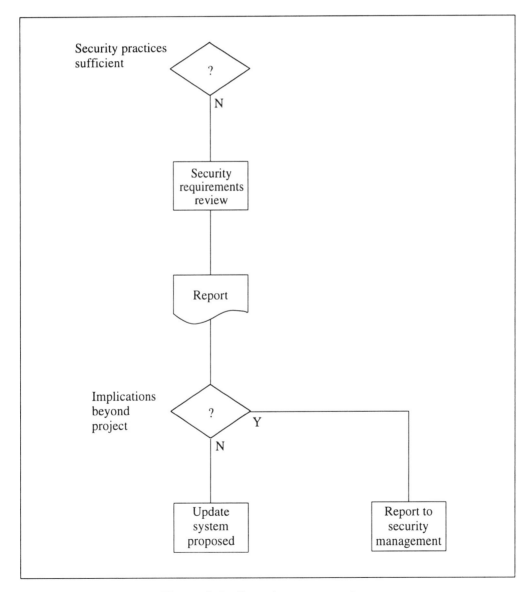

Figure 3.6   Security repercussions

Confidentiality

- Which requirements relate to confidentiality?
- Where will confidentiality be important in the new system?
- Who needs to see the data?
- What access rights will each category of user have?
- What could happen if the system gave users access to more data than they need for their work, e.g. fraud?
- How will users be able to access the data? Consider:
  - viewing on screens;
  - printing reports;
  - copying to diskettes or other media.
  - Is any of the data particularly sensitive, for example data identified as potentially causing serious loss if divulged to a rival? If so can it be restricted to certain users only without making the system difficult to use?
- Is any of the data subject to legal controls, for example, data protection legislation? If so, what is being done about it?
- Is data input from any source which might be insecure, e.g. a remote site?
- How secure are the networks used by the company? Will the level of security be sufficient for the system being developed?
- What happens to printed reports with confidential data?
- What hardware will be used for the system? How secure is it and its operating system?
- What are the baseline controls of the installation? Can they be used, at least as a partial solution?
- If the system is a replacement, what access control measures are in place at he moment? Can they be reused or adapted for the new system?

Integrity

- Which requirements relate to integrity?
- How important will integrity be in the new system?
- What systems operations can affect the integrity of data? In particular the following should be considered.
  - Who can amend, insert and delete data?
  - What sort of data is affected?
- What benefits would be gained by recording changes to data?
- For what categories of data should a record of changes be maintained?
- How should changes to data be recorded and what should be recorded?

- Who will be able to access the record of changes to data?

- Is any data known to be especially important? Could special safeguards be considered for this data only?

- How will the system draw attention to potential problems of integrity?

- How is data verified?

- Are the parameters for verification (e.g. master files) under user control? How will the system ensure that a division of responsibilities is maintained?

- Can batch input controls be used? If so, who would check them?

- Does any data come from an external source such as another company? Is so, consider:

  - how can we be sure that it is valid at source?

  - how can we be sure that it is valid when it reaches our system?

- Does the system provide any scope for fraud? Is so, what controls might be considered which would:

  - provide evidence of tampering;

  - show if money is being diverted;

  - indicate who is responsible;

  - show when this happens as quickly as possible;

  - produce a record which could be used in a prosecution?

- If the system is a replacement, can any controls in the previous system be used in the new one? If the previous system was a manual one, the fact that a computer is now being used should not mean that controls are scrapped.

- Based on experience of similar systems, are there any controls which would be suitable here?

- Would an audit of the data be useful? If so, how often should this be done and what would be the best way of doing it?

- What backup strategy would reduce the risk of data being permanently destroyed or wrongly modified?

Availability

Most computer installations have a recovery policy for their systems which will allow resumption of work after a delay. Will this policy be adequate for the new system? Also, an acceptable level of response may have been agreed for other systems. Will this still hold true for the new system? These are important questions and it is important that computer operations are not unwittingly put in the position of providing an inadequate service because of lack of information.

- Are there any operations in the system, or any periods when availability is particularly important?

- From what is known of the system, are there any functions which are more likely than others to be prone to problems of availability?

- What volume of transactions is anticipated for the new system? When will heavy use be made of it?

- What service level is demanded? Is it feasible?

- Can the service level requested be maintained with the hardware and software currently in use in the installation?

- Does any function need particularly fast response? For example, some systems such as those used in libraries need fast access of records for inquiries. Can this be catered for by efficient systems design or special software?

- Are the recovery requirements met by existing arrangements? If not, what can be done to meet them?

- Are there any networks or parts of the system outside of our control? What problems of availability do they present?

Reporting the findings

The author of this report should try to present information in such a way as it can be easily incorporated into the system proposal. Alternative solutions may be recommended. If there seems to be little to choose between them, give the advantages and disadvantages of each. The report should also point out where expensive solutions might be needed or where changes to current security policy and arrangements might be required.

The report should not be more detailed that the system proposal since the solutions it recommends will probably be included in it. Where possible, existing countermeasures should be used or adapted. The temptation to look for new technology should be resisted unless the threats justify it.

If there is a case for drastically changing the companies security arrangements, it will obviously require further research. For example, if a new system needs a far higher level of access control than others, a case may be made for looking for a PC access control device. A further case might then be made for reviewing all PC security within the company in the hope that a product could be found which would serve not only the system under development but others as well. The report would then serve as input to another investigation, related to but not strictly part of the current project. The project manager would need to keep a close check on its progress to make sure that it would not unacceptably delay the system under development.

The following checklist should be consulted when considering the contents of this report.

- Can the security requirements be met by systems development *per se*? For example, if the system is easy to use and has effective, well designed validation procedures, an intelligent and intelligible help facility, it is less likely that problems of integrity will occur. The following areas of the project should be examined closely:

  - validation, controls, access;

  - documentation;

- database selection;

- training;

- change control procedures.

• Where can traditional controls, such as those used in accounting, be introduced? How can the system make sure that they are not ignored or overridden?

• For each security requirement which has been identified - what has been the practice in other systems and what is the normal practice within the company?

• Can current security measures be adapted if not adequate in their present form?

• What would the consequences be if current security measures were changed? How would computer operations, users and other computer systems be affected?

• If there is more than one solution to a security requirement, what are the advantages and disadvantages of each?

• Which will be most suitable for the system?

• Are any of the following necessary:

  - new hardware or software (e.g. security devices);

  - changes to agreed service levels;

  - changes to recovery procedures;

  - limitations in links with other computer installations, for example if access via a network may have to be curtailed;

  - operational procedures;

  - changes within the user department?

If the report recommends any of these, they should not be included in the system proposal. The project manager will decide how best to follow them up.

• Given the timescales for the project, what will be the effect of waiting for a solution to be implemented? This will apply if the internal systems controls are not a remedy and current security methods fall short. Consider also:

  - are there any temporary measures which might provide an acceptable level of security for the time being;

  - what would be the effect of leaving this security function out of the system for the time being?

Review

The documents produced during the Definition Phase should be reviewed before work begins on the next phase. There is no need to complete work on the project plan before beginning the system proposal. It will almost certainly be altered when the system proposal is written.

Project plan

The plan should be reviewed to ensure that it provides a feasible means of controlling the project. It will be reviewed as the project progresses. Change is normal as the details of the project becomes clearer and as new tasks are identified.

- Are the contents comprehensive in that they cover all activities throughout the project?

- Does the plan cover the whole of the project? In particular:

  - Does every phase have a start and end date?

  - Is the total time required for each phase estimated?

  - Are the activities for each phase defined, with approximate timescales?

- Is the current phase treated in detail so that the plan can be used to manage staff and their work?

- Can the source of all activities be traced back to the documents produced during the previous phase? If not, what extra activities are there and is it clear why they are being introduced and what is their bearing on the project as a whole?

- Has anything been omitted?

- Are there any potential clashes as far as allocation of resources is concerned? Staff who may be working on another project should be considered.

- Does the implementation period coincide with any other dates, for example, a time of extra activity in the user department?

- Are the estimates for staff and times reasonable? What are the bases for the estimates, e.g. similar project?

- Is there an element of contingency in the timescales?

- Is there an externally imposed deadline? Have the estimated dates simply been calculated back from it? If so, how realistic are?

- Has the extent of user involvement, dates, etc, been agreed?

- Is there evidence that external resources (software, people, etc.) will be available when required?

- Where one task is shown to be dependent upon another, what will be the consequences of any delay in completing the first task?

- Are there any activities which are parallel activities? For example if a prototype is going to be used as part of the development alongside 'in house' development, is the relationship between these activities clear?

- Does the plan show how communications with all interested parties will be maintained? Consider users, other members of the computer department, external companies, those responsible for other computer systems and those providing expert assistance such as security and quality specialists.

This same checklist can be used when reviewing the plan after it has been revised during the later phases of the project.

Quality plan

- Does the plan correspond to the recommended contents given above?
- Does it meet the approval of quality assurance staff?
- Will the output of the reviews be a useful source for improving the current level of quality?
- Do the reviews and inspections prescribed fit in with the timescales and activities in the project plan?
- Are the number of reviews and techniques used acceptable given the importance of the project, time constraints, etc?
- Are trained resources available to carry out inspections?

Prototype definition

- Is the prototype limited to all or part of the functions in the system proposal?
- If it is a part of the system only, is it a discrete part which can be managed without unduly impinging on the rest of the development?
- Is its place in the project and its significance for the rest of the project quite clear?
- Are the estimated resource requirements reasonable and available?
- Is it clear what the aims of the prototype are and are these aims compatible with the aims of the new system?
- Is it clear when the prototype will be ready, when its evaluation will be complete and when it will be dispensed with? Even if the prototype is going to be converted into part of the system, there will still be a time when it ceases to be a prototype.
- Is it obvious that benefits of the prototype will justify the time, money and effort being put into it?

Package evaluation plan

- Can all the requirements be traced to the statement of requirements and other source documents?
- Do the dates and staffing requirements clash with any in the project plan?
- Does the completion of the evaluation make the completion of the project on time less likely?
- Is the division between 'in-house' development and the functions of the package made clear, in so far as they are known at this date?
- Is the number of packages being compared in the evaluation sufficient for useful comparisons to be made but not excessive?
- Are the products available in a form suitable for evaluation? A demonstration copy is not sufficient.

System proposal

- Are the contents comprehensive, covering those recommended above?
- Can every feature of the system be traced back to the statement of requirements?
- Are there any omissions or parts of the system which do not precisely mirror the requirements?
- Are the documents and diagrams in compliance with project standards?
- Have all other relevant source documents been taken into account, for example the system justification?
- Is the proposed system technically feasible? Consider the following.
  - Volumes of data, including input and output.
  - Response time.
  - Access time.
  - Peak processing requirements.
  - Human interfaces.
  - Operational requirements.
- Does it now appear that new software, hardware or skills will be required which were not identified during Initiation?
- Do the cost estimates calculated during Initiation still appear realistic?
- Are the arrangements for storing data in archives adequate in view of the anticipated life of the system and the anticipated life of the data? Some kinds of data may still be required when the system is replaced.
- Are the levels of service (including such matters as systems recovery and response) feasible both technically and from the point of view of costs?
- Are the interfaces with other systems defined showing how other systems will be affected?
- Does the proposal show a clear delineation between functions such as those of managers and other staff?
- Will the system controls provide rapid and clear evidence of abuse of the system and accidental corruption?
- Is there an audit trail? If so, is it comprehensive, enabling transactions to be traced all the way through the system? Will it enable us to discover precisely;
  - when each transaction is performed;
  - at which stage and during which process each transaction is performed;
  - who is responsible?
- Is it apparent from the proposal who will be responsible (by function) for authorising the following:

- running programs or requesting that programs should be run, including special processing such as year-end processing;

- receiving reports;

- granting access rights;

- restoring data from archives?

- Will the system conform to the law when it goes live? Have measures been taken to make sure that it will, such as registration under data protection legislation?

- In view of the contents of the system proposal, will any other systems be affected in any way not envisaged during Initiation?

- Will any changes to the project plan will have to be made, for example, timescales, staffing, software, training?

- If a package is being evaluated for some of the system, is it clear which functions will be covered by it and how it will fit in with the rest of the system and other system?

- Have any diagrams or other visual aid, been used? Will they be understood by all who read the system proposal?

Security Requirements Review

- Is the starting point for the review one or more of the requirements in the statement of requirements?

- Do any of the things considered in the review stray from the project in hand?

- Are the recommended solutions practical and based on experience?

- If a temporary solution is recommended, what risks are involved and for how long will it be necessary to wait for a permanent countermeasure?

- Are the recommended solutions feasible and effective in view of the likelihood of a breach of security and its potential business impact?

- Is it clear what the implications for the project are in terms of:

  - software;

  - hardware;

  - time;

  - costs;

  - training;

  - systems design?

- How will other systems be affected?

- If the solutions imply changes to working practices for users or computer staff, are they acceptable?

- If there are any implications for current security policy and practices, what are the changes and how will they be made?

- If alternatives are given, are the merits of each made clear?

- Are any other documents affected by this review, for example, the statement of requirements or the package evaluation plan? Although the security requirements review is considered as a source mainly for the system proposal, its contents may also determine precisely what is required from a package. For example, a type of management control might be needed or the package might have to work with a specific make of access control device.

End of phase

The Definition phase ends when the following documents have been reviewed and finalised.

- The system proposal must be accepted by users and other interested parties, such as computer operations, as the basis for a viable solution to the requirements.

- The project plan must be seen to provide a realistic framework for controlling the project and for ensuring that quality objectives are met.

- Where any implications have been discovered which go beyond the scope of the project, the project manager has taken steps to make sure something is done about them.

- A prototype has been defined, if a prototype is going to be used.

- If some or all of the project has been earmarked for packaged software, a plan for the evaluation has been drawn up.

The agreement of the users to the system proposal, prototype and package evaluation plan is essential.

4 System specification

The broad definition of the data and functions contained in the system proposal is now converted into a detailed model and description of the new system. The level of detail is such that all attributes of every item of data are specified; all processing is described step by step. The outcome is a single document called the system specification. It encompasses two separate activities each producing distinct documents, the package evaluation report and the prototype analysis.

The activities in this phase are the ones which are dealt with in great detail in many books on system development. Here, we concentrate on the end result, i.e. the system specification, rather than the process by which you arrive at it. There are many ways of designing systems but the end result should be a document from which the system can be created and which will serve as a detailed, accurate description.

The first step towards converting the system into a physical reality is taken here. The description of data within the system specification has to be communicated to the data management specialists so that it can be checked and integrated with other data structures. If possible a model of the data structures, perhaps for use as a test environment, can be created at the end of this phase or during the next one.

During this phase, methodologies are at their most useful. Indeed, the system specification can consist almost entirely of diagrams and formal lists. If you have used a methodology during the Definition phase, you can easily build on the documents developed then, converting them and adding detail. Of course, you may wish to make limited use of a methodology, for example with data modelling at a fairly high level only. Methodologies can be used eclectically and, if this suits you, why not? The only difficulty you are likely to meet is deciding precisely to what extent you should use the methodology.

Data dictionaries and CASE tools also become very useful now, relieving the project team of much of the drudgery which used to be associated with this activity. A good CASE tool should also assist the project team in its reviews by automatically ensuring that one type of diagram is fully compatible with another.

Project planning is fairly straightforward unless you have elected to evaluate an applications package or to use a prototype. However, the benefits of defining the prototype or planning the evaluation during the last phase will now be apparent. The project manager can at least monitor the progress of these two activities and the quality of the work against these source documents. The final version of the system specification will, of course, depend on the outcome of these two activities. The project manager will make sure that the information needed to complete the systems specification is available as soon as possible (*see* Figure 4.1).

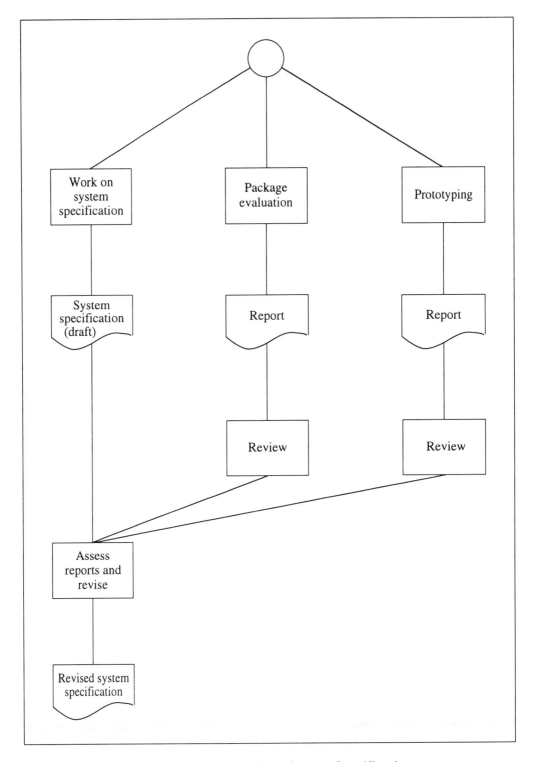

Figure 4.1   Sources of the System Specification

Other difficulties may arise. During the detailed analysis, the requirements might change or a potential security risk might be uncovered. Perhaps this will mean reviewing the system proposal or even the statement of requirements. If a security problem emerges, it may be advisable to look at the potential business impact and if the threat is a serious one, introduce countermeasures. Some prototypes, too, point to a way of meeting the original requirements which had not been thought of.

Probably the worst scenario is that a package evaluation shows that the products under review just do not measure up to requirements and that either another will have to be evaluated or the system will have to be developed entirely 'in-house'. The chance of any of these happening is slight if sufficient care has been taken during the Initiation and Definition phases. In the case of a failed package evaluation, damage will be limited if the requirements have been well defined. Even if you are left with no choice but to proceed along the 'in-house' route, the requirements can be translated into a revised system proposal and system specification (*see* Figure 4.2).

User involvement is now about detail. The project team will want to know precisely what potential values the data might have, exactly what validation is needed, just how the reports are going to be laid out. If calculations now performed manually are going to be part of the system, full details should have been made available already. If not, they must be set down now with worked examples which can be translated into computer code later on. Therefore, it is essential that the project manager makes sure that users are available for consultation and also for checking to see that the project team has understood properly.

Sometimes users are involved in the detailed design of the system and can provide valuable assistance, especially in reviews. If the team is using a methodology, it will help if such users have already been trained in the methodology. A reading knowledge of, for example, SSADM is not difficult to acquire and will mean that the users are not mystified by the documents they are asked to comment on. Otherwise, the project manager will have to make sure that the bulk of the documentation is in natural language.

Phase initiation

Work should only begin on this phase when the system proposal has been reviewed and accepted by all interested parties, especially the users, as the basis for the system. Any other documents from the Definition phase which are source documents for this phase, namely a package evaluation plan or a prototype definition should also be ready.

Sometimes, agreement takes a long time, especially if the user who has to accept the system proposal on behalf of the user department is unavailable. The project manager may decide to go ahead, albeit with caution, especially if working to a tight deadline. The decision will take into account the probability of agreement being forthcoming and the consequences of delivering the system late.

* Is it likely that full user agreement will be forthcoming? The risks of doing so are less if, for example, the user representatives who have been working with the project manager up to now agree that agreement is little more than a formality.

* What will happen of the system is not delivered on time?

* What will the project team do if they do not carry on with the project?

* What would the consequences be if changes to the system were requested?

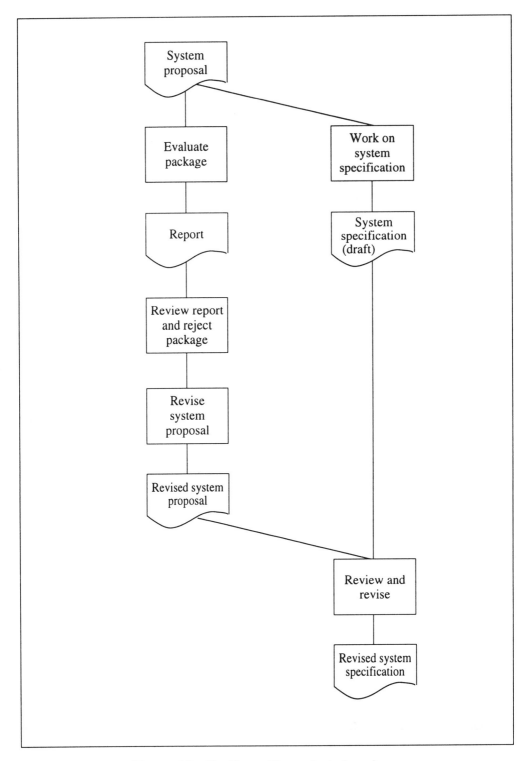

Figure 4.2   Dealing with a rejected package

- Are there any parts of the system where changes are less likely to be required than others? Is it possible to proceed with them?
- Is a package evaluation being contemplated? Can this begin without full agreement to the system proposal?
- Is a prototype being used? If so, can work begin on this in isolation?

Obviously, the project manager should insist on agreement being reached as soon as possible.

Documents

Apart from the revised project plan, the main document in a straightforward, 'in-house' development is the system specification. It may be written mainly in natural language but will almost certainly include a large number of methodology diagrams, showing the processing and data of the system together, file layouts, tables and so on. The author should be mindful of future generations of systems development staff, who will have to maintain it, and of those who work on other systems which might access the data contained in this one. If you use a methodology, the constituent parts of the specification can easily be reviewed separately and from a different perspective. Reviewing parts of the system and following these with a complete review is sometimes a convenient way of proceeding at this stage, especially if the system is large.

The two main optional documents are the package evaluation report and the prototype analysis. The first makes a clear recommendation about the selection of a package. If one is chosen there should be enough information for the project team to be able to define the interfaces with the rest of the system. The prototype analysis should prove that the aims of the prototype have been met and show how they can be brought into the completed system.

Assuming data management is performed by experts, the project manager will want to be able to inform them of the requirements for the system under development. The data management specialists will look at the data from a different perspective to the project team. They will want to see that it complies with standards, that the data dictionary entries will make sense and that the structures are feasible and efficient. From this they will create the data structures. Many computer departments have a formal procedure for this. Here we look at the contents of a data management specification which could be used to communicate with data management staff.

Main documents
- Project plan
    - Target audience: all those working on the project.
- System specification
    - Target audience: users;
        project staff;
        computer department management;
        other systems development staff.

This is a key document.

Optional Documents

- Package evaluation report
  - Target audience: users;

    project staff;

    computer centre management.

- Prototype analysis
  - Target audience: users;

    project staff;

    computer centre management.

- Data management specification
  - Target audience: data management staff.

The system specification will not be complete until the optional documents have been reviewed and their impact on the system ascertained.

Project plan

The project plan should be reviewed at the beginning of every phase, to see how closely the estimates were met and to revise where necessary. In addition, the detailed planning of the current phase should be carried out now.

The project as a whole

- How accurate were the estimates for the Definition phase?

- Does the content of the system proposal or the other documents produced during Definition indicate that the original estimates for this phase are still likely to be accurate?

- In view of this, are the estimates for the remainder of the project likely to need revision?

- Are the changes likely to cause any problems, for example, because of time constraints on the project?

- Have any other factors emerged which might have a bearing on estimates for the project? For example, staff might be unavailable.

The current phase

- What activities are planned for this phase?

- What documents will be produced?

- Who will participate in each activity?

- How long will each activity take to complete and when will it begin and end?

- Is a methodology being used? If so,
  - are all staff properly trained;
  - what documents will be produced and to what level of detail;
  - how will staff working on related activities communicate and share information?
- Is a CASE tool being used? If so,
  - are staff fully trained;
  - are there enough copies of the software;
  - what provision is there for ensuring version control, especially if there is shared access?
- Which users will be involved?
- What will their roles be?
- When will they be available?
- Is a prototype being created? If so,
  - what is its bearing on the rest of the development (in particular how will it affect the design of the system);
  - will it be merged with the rest of the system and, if so, when?
- Are packages being evaluated? If so, when will details of interfaces with the rest of the system be available?

System specification

This document contains a description of everything the system does – processes, data, controls, relationship with other systems. If an applications package is an integral part of the system that will be described here as well, although not always in the same detail. A good package will be sufficiently well documented for its own documentation to either be integrated into the system specification or to be used as a source.

The system specification serves two main purposes: it is the source of subsequent development – all programming, testing, evaluation and system documentation derive from it; it is also the main record of the system and should be written with a view to providing maintenance staff with a clear description of the system's functions. Therefore, it should always be kept up to date throughout the life of the system. Like other documents subject to revision, it is wise to use a method of version control and to make the amendment history a feature of the specification.

The following information should be included at the front of the specification by way of introduction.

- Identity: name of the author, date written, current version number.
- Amendment history: the author, date, version number and brief description of every amendment.
- Context: identity of source documents, related documents (e.g. of documents belonging to an applications package, related systems and subsystems).

- Introduction: a summary of the chief functions of the system. This should allow the reader to understand how it works at a high level both as software and as a business process. A high level data flow diagram should be included and other methodology diagrams where appropriate.

- Dictionary information: the identity of the data dictionary and catalogue of programs in the system, (assuming they will be used).

Content

The checklists given below are a guide to the main topics to be considered. Every systems development department has its chosen method of writing system specifications so how you actually express these contents, i.e. in prose, in diagrams, through a methodology or by a combination of these means is not discussed here.

Data

- What data structures are needed? Give their identities and, unless a data dictionary is used, a description.

- What type of structures are they (e.g. database files, indexed sequential, serial files)?

- What is the sequence of each data structure?

- What media are used (e.g. EDS, CD-ROM, magnetic tape)?

- Which structures exist already and do they need any modification for this system? If so, does this imply any changes to other systems?

- Which external data structures are accessed?

- What is the size of each data structure (including original size, anticipated growth, maximum size)?

- How is each data structure accessed? Give all access paths.

- What is the source of each file?

- What is the destination of each output file?

- Who owns the data (i.e. makes decisions about access)?

- What is the identity of each element of data (field, data item)? Unless a data dictionary is used, descriptions should be provided.

- What is the size and type of each data element?

- What range of values or permitted values are valid for each?

- What is the base value of each?

- What cross validation of elements of data between files is needed? Note mutually exclusive categories such as 'male' and 'pregnant'.

- What data is associated with or dependent on other data in any way?

- What parameters are used? Give the size, permitted values and significance for the system of each.

- What data is held on other systems, including data accessed on remote computers? In particular:

  - who owns it;

  - how is it updated and when;

  - how will it be accessed;

  - what would be the effect of any change to the format or permitted values of the data;

  - how will any such changes be communicated to the owners of the system under development?

- What is the best way of presenting each data structure and element of data for the readers of the specification? Obviously, if there is a method prescribed for the project, it should be used. Output from a data dictionary can also be used if it is presentable and complete. Unless there are strict controls on changes to a data dictionary, simply referring to it in the specification can easily lead to the processing sect ion becoming out of date.

- What are the security requirements for each structure and data element? User classes for read and write access should be given if they are an integral part of a database management system. Any other special restrictions should be given here.

Processing

- What is the function of each process?

- How is it initiated?

- When is a process initiated, e.g. ad hoc, monthly, yearly?

- What data is accessed by it and how is it accessed?

- What is output from the process (e.g. an updated file, a completed calculation, an intermediate result)?

- What happens to the output of each process after the process has been completed?

- What determines that a process is complete?

- What happens if an error or unexpected condition is encountered during the process? Note in particular:

  - what error messages will be generated;

  - who will receive them;

  - what will happen to error messages generated by the compiler, operating system, proprietary database software etc. – in other words by anything other than the application under development.

Users should not be expected to understand system generated error codes and the accompanying displays which are very technical and may include machine code. The information such displays convey may be valuable in tracking down the source of the error but this is not something users will be expected to do. Users should only have to deal with a brief plainly-worded message in natural language, telling them what the error is and what they need to do.

The same, of course, applies to validation and other message which the new system will provide. It may be desirable to link the error messages to the on-line 'help' facility so that, if the users are still stuck they can be advised as to what further steps they can take.

- What should the users do if the system fails completely, for example, in the event of a sudden loss of power or communications?

- What will be the effect on processing so far carried out if an error occurs?

- What other processes are called by this one?

- What other processes call this one?

- How does this process interface with others (i.e. parameters)? If an applications package is part of the system, the interface should be considered here.

- What processing does this process share with others? Is there a case for writing a subroutine called by others?

- What performance requirements are there for this process? How will the way the processing is actually carried out enable them to be met?

- Is any processing restricted to certain categories of user? If so, how can we ensure that this requirement is actually reflected in the system?

- If some kind of authorisation is needed to perform this process, how is that given?

- Is any human intervention needed? If so, what has to be done and how does the process communicate?

- What is the process broken down into simple stages? Give details of each step of each calculation.

- What logging requirements are there for each process? Take care to define what a transaction is in logging terms.

- What locking has to be performed when a data structure is accessed?

- What screens are needed?

- What is the layout of each?

- What data is accessed by each screen?

- What categories of user can access each screen?

- What access rights to each element of data on the screens does each category of user have?

- What processing can be invoked from each screen?

- Which validation is required on input screens?

- What messages can be communicated to the user?

- What triggers off each message?
- What can the user do on receiving each message?
- Which other screens can be called from each screen?
- Which screens are linked so that one normally follows the other (as distinct from being called voluntarily by the user)?
- How can the user abandon processing and what happens to the data on the screen?
- How will the user obtain help?
- What system-wide help is available?
- What help is available for the current screen and processing only?
- What are the requirements for operating systems and compilers?
- What processes produce printed reports?
- Where are reports printed?
- Who can order each report?
- Who can receive each report?
- What are the volumes and number of copies of each report?
- What special stationery is required for reports?
- If end-user reporting is a feature of the system, how is it to be invoked?
- How is end-user reporting controlled, e.g. access rights, limitations on processing capabilities?

Layouts for each screen and report should normally be provided.

Security
- What special security requirements have been identified?
- How will confidential access be provided, especially online access?
- How will confidential reports be distributed?
- What system controls are needed, e.g. an audit trail?
- What controls are embedded in each process?
- How can the integrity of the controls by guaranteed?
- How will controls be checked?
- What controls actually inhibit further processing until someone intervenes? How is such intervention performed?
- What procedures and methods are there for checking the audit trail?
- What processes are there for restoring the system in the event of a failure? If a standard recovery plan is in place, this should be dealt with as part of the plan.

- What procedures for taking backup copies of data structures are there?
- What data is placed in archives and how is this achieved? When is it placed there and for how long is it kept?

Operational operations

Computer operations need to be aware of the effect of the system on hardware and software and to consider staffing requirements. They also need to understand how the system fits in with others. Such information should be available now, although the detailed planning of the suites of programs and so on cannot be undertaken yet.

- What processes will be run by computer operations?
- How is the system accessed and when must it be available?
- What remote access to the system will there be?
- How does this system access others and when will these other systems be available?
- How will other systems be affected by this one, for example, in terms of use of storage, hardware and software and changes to processing?
- On what other systems does this one depend?
- What other systems depend on this one?
- Within this system, which processes depend on this one?
- Which current data structures will be affected by this system?
- What is the anticipated growth rate of the new data structures?

Redundancies

- What computer systems, processing and data structures will be replaced by this one?
- What storage will be released as a result of this system being introduced?

Package evaluation report

Assuming you decided to evaluate one or more applications packages, the report should aim to show the extent to which the aims of the package evaluation have been met and make a recommendation about purchase. It should also contain enough information to show how the package will fit in with the rest of the system. In this way, the system specification can be completed.

- Which package, if any, is to be recommended? Why is it the best one?
- Have all the requirements contained in the package evaluation plan been met? If not,
    - which requirements have not been meet;
    - which packages did not meet them;
    - is the recommended package still acceptable even though the requirement is not met?

- Have all the points raised in the package evaluation plan been dealt with? They should be addressed in the report.
- Which packages are produced in accordance with ISO 9000?
- Are there any doubts as to the viability of any of the companies?
- Which package, if any, appears to be the best choice?
- Which language is it written in?
- When will it be available?
- What types of data structures does it use?
- What are the sizes, capacities, expected growth rate, sequence access methods and security of the data structures?
- What are the data elements, including size, permitted value, and security?
- What methods of accessing the data is provided with the package?
- Are there any problems in interfacing between the package and the rest of the system, e.g. operational considerations?
- Do any of the current plans for enhancing the package have an impact on the data structure, access methods and so on, in such a way as to imply changes to the 'in-house' part of the system?
- Are all the facilities in the recommended package actually present or are they based on promises for the future? If the latter, what is the basis for believing with confidence that the facilities will be introduced as and when promised?

This report will be used to reach a decision about purchasing the package. Its contents should enable the project team to assess the impact of the package before the decision is made. The extent to which detailed work is done will depend on the project manager's opinion as to the likelihood of the report's recommendation being accepted.

Prototype analysis

The prototype definition states what the prototype should achieve. The prototype analysis describes what has actually been achieved when the exercise has finished. Since the object of a prototype can vary greatly from a scaled-down version of the complete system to an attempt to clarify thinking on a discrete part of the system, the impact on the system specification will also vary. It is possible that a considerable part of the system specification will be derived from this document.

- What were the goals of the prototype definition and to what extent have they been met?
- If it is felt that further work is needed, what does this imply in terms of:
  - revision to the aims of the prototype;
  - staffing levels, effort, time and costs?
- What parts of the system have been the subject of the prototype and what are the implications for the rest of the system now that the prototype has been completed?

- Is it intended to convert the prototype into the system or part of the system, or else to use it in order to make decisions about the system's functions? In either case,

  - what are the sizes, capacities, expected growth rate, sequence access methods and security of the data structures;

  - what are the data elements, including size, permitted values and security;

  - what are the implications for the new system's processing?

Is the prototype is being converted so that it can be incorporated into the system? If so:

  - what modifications are needed to the processing and data structures of the model, so that it conforms to standards and can be integrated with the rest of the system;

  - what has to be done to make it comply with security requirements and agreed performance levels;

  - what has to be done to transfer the data?

- If the prototype is a model of a discrete part of the system, how does it link up with the rest?

- What other implications for the new system are there, for example, performance, security, interfaces, size?

- Are there any results which might affect the Definition phase, requiring amendment to the system proposal?

- Are the users satisfied with the prototype completely? If the aim of the prototype has not been met, what further measures could be taken? It may not be necessary to reject the prototype if it can be demonstrated that the problem is with the prototype only and will not be present in the live system. For example, if the performance of the model is judged too slow, can we be certain that this is something which will be put right?

- Is the prototype resilient within the limitations of its planned capabilities?

- If some or all of the aims of the prototype have not been met, what are they and how significant are they? What can be done to improve matters? Were the limitations of the prototyping language or lack of familiarity with it to blame in any way?

The system specification should be amended in the light of this report.

Data management specification

The questions given here assume that this is a separate document for data management specialists who will create the physical structures. The data structures will have been reviewed as part of the review of the system specification. Now a document requesting that the data management staff should accept them as valid. This means that you need to give more information than just the proposed name for the data elements and structures, together with a description of size, format and so on. This is important information and needs to be conveyed accurately and in terms familiar to data management staff. If you are using a certain proprietary type of database, it will have its own method of presentation, nomenclature and so on. If this is what the data management staff require, the project manager should see that they are provided with it.

The data management experts need to make sure that it will fit in with the rest of the data they are responsible for and that it will be able to perform the function it is meant to. What is needed is not a rehash of the system specification but a few, pertinent hard facts and figures about the way the data will be used and what is expected of it.

The checklist given below is necessarily general but can be used as a basis for creating your own checklists for your data environment.

DATABASES

- What databases will the system use?
- What type of databases are there, e.g. relational?
- Are the databases proprietary such as INGRES or TOTAL?
- What function will the database perform and what sort of data will it hold?
- How much space will the database require when the system is implemented?
- At what rate do you anticipate the database will grow?
- What is the estimated maximum size?
- What security requirements are there?
- What relationship do the databases have with each other and with other, existing databases?
- Who is the owner?

DATA STRUCTURES

- What data structures will the system use?
- If they are part of a database, to which database does each belong?
- What function will each perform and what sort of data (in business terms) will it hold?
- What name is recommended for each?
- What security requirements are there?
- What is the initial size on implementation?
- What is the anticipated growth rate?
- What is the estimated maximum size?
- What is the sequence of the data within each structure?
- Who is the owner?
- What is the relationship of each structure with others, for example, common access keys, hierarchical structure?
- How will the structures be accessed?
- What constitutes a record?
- How is a record identified? If there is a unique key, state what it is.

DATA ELEMENTS

- What are the data elements?
- To which structures do they belong?
- What function will each perform and what sort of information (in business terms) will it hold?
- What name is recommended for each?
- What is the size and type of each? Type means data type, e.g. packed decimal.
- What is the base value of each data element?
- What values can the element hold, e.g. range or permitted values?
- What security is required?
- Who owns each data element?

GENERAL

- Are there performance criteria which affect any of the data?
- What data will be replaced by this data?
- What databases, structures and elements are amended versions of data which exists already?
- Can any of the structures be set up without affecting any other existing data structures? If not, how would the new structures be created? This will be planned during the next phase but the data management team should be given early warning.
- When is a version of the data structure required by, e.g. for testing?
- How many test versions are needed?
- Have any data protection or other legal implications been noted? If so, what steps are being taken to ensure compliance with the law?
- Is a data dictionary in use? If the project team is meant to provide input for it, it should be done now, at least as a draft version.

Review

System specification

The system specification should be reviewed for completion and comprehensiveness. It is also important to check that it is correct.

- Do the contents match those of the source documents, especially the system proposal, with no alterations, omissions or additions?
- Do the contents indicate that the checklist for writing the specification has been followed? If there are project standards, have they been obeyed?
- Have the standards for the methodology been adhered to?

- Is sufficient information given about the data elements and data structures so that,
  - all can be readily identified by name and description;
  - the sizes and values are known;
  - no security requirements have been overlooked;
  - the effect of the system's processing on the data can be easily discovered;
  - a data management specification can be prepared from it?
- Is all the processing defined so that program specifications, batch jobs, user and operations documentation, etc, can all be prepared?
- Is there any data which is not used by the processing and which therefore may be redundant?
- Is it apparent how the system will interface with others?
- If a package has been used, is it apparent how that will fit in with the rest of the system?
- Do the interfaces imply any possible loss of security?
- Can we be sure that remote users will get the service they are supposed to get, given the network access being provided?
- Are there any implications for other systems, e.g. consequential amendments?
- Is it clear that the backup arrangements would enable the level of recovery required by the system?
- Will the arrangements for sending data to archives permit useful and easy access when needed?
- Can the specification be used as an input document for the company's disaster recovery plan.
- Will the detailed security provisions provide the level of security required in the system proposal?
- Is there anything which suggests the system could be made more efficient, bearing in mind the level of service which it should provide?
- Is it clear how controls should work and that all those described in the specification are genuine, effective controls?
- Is there anything which suggests that the security measures prescribed in earlier documents may not be sufficient?
- Are the estimates for volumes, peak processing times access time and other figures with a bearing on the level of service still valid? Would it be feasible to revise them?
- Does the content of the specification imply that revision to the project plan is needed?
- Are the original cost estimates still valid?
- Have any new requirements emerged which might imply that more training or new software or hardware are needed?
- Do any of the statements in the specification contradict each other?

- Are calculations specified correctly? It should be possible to test them by working through each and comparing the result with a worked example provided by a user and calculated by the current method employed in the user department.

- Is good business practice followed in the processing, for example is there a clear division between the access provisions for supervisors with special responsibilities and other staff?

- Are master files and sensitive data only accessible by those authorised to see them, including those using end-user reporting?

- Is all input validated and clearly shown to be valid and complete through controls?

- Do the input controls include batch totals, range checks and checks for reasonable values, where such checks might be appropriate?

- Can processes which fail because of control checks be corrected? Is there any risk of this being used to circumvent controls?

- If data is sent to or received from other systems, is it reconciled for integrity?

- Are the controls sufficient to make sure that there is a record of changes to data structures if this is desirable?

- Do the controls provide an adequate record of volumes and errors?

- If an audit trail has been used, is it easily accessible but only to those who need it?

- Does it provide clear evidence of errors or malpractice?

- Is every error clearly reported and directed at the appropriate staff (users, computer department, etc.)?

- Are all messages clear, unambiguous and consistent? If there is a system-wide or company-wide policy, has it been adhered to?

- Has anything emerged which suggests compliance with the law might require further action, for example, with data protection legislation?

- Are all names and descriptions used, sensible, intelligible and in conformance with standards?

- Is there any redundancy in any of the data structures or elements?

- Are the data structures well-designed and capable of providing the level of access required?

- Will the data and processing be valid for the anticipated life of the system? For example, where monetary data is represented, how is inflation likely to affect it? Currency is obviously an important factor here.

- Are the types of data suitable for the operations which will be performed on them by the system? Take dates for example, if you ever want to sort by date it is better to use a YYYYMMDD sequence. Note that century has been included here as part of the date.

- Do the data structures provide a balanced solution with regard to:
  - economy of storage;
  - ease of access;
  - ease of processing;
  - efficiency of processing?

  In other words, has the data been optimised and, if so, is it really the best solution for everyone using or operating the system?
- Is there any unfamiliar hardware, software, databases, operating systems, etc? If so, what are the implications both for the project and for the computer department and users?

Package evaluation report

- Have the terms of reference, special selection criteria and other rules and standards been adhered to?
- Does the report demonstrate clearly why one solution is preferable to others?
- Does the report provide evidence for its findings, for example, it is not based on promises?
- Are the features considered by the evaluation all traceable to our requirements?
- Has the author of the report taken due account of other sources specified by the project manager, for example, checklists provided in this book?
- Does the report provide enough information for all those who will be reading it, including users and computer operations?
- Is it clear what the implications are for the rest of the system under development and other systems?
- Does the report suggest any potential problem areas with the package, for example, it might be slow or not up to the required level of security? How can these be remedied?
- Are there any similar problem areas with the supplier? For example, there may be possible delays in making the product available or the company may be located in a different time zone making communication difficult.
- If any such potential problem areas have been identified, are any solutions offered?
- Are any changes to the system required as a result?
- Is every advantage and disadvantage listed in the report traceable to our requirements?

Prototype analysis

- Does the report show to what extent the aims of the prototype have been met, including any shortcomings?
- Does the report focus on the practical use of the exercise? In other words, what should we do as a result of the prototype analysis?

- Have any changes to the system been recommended? If so, what are their implications for the project as a whole? Are they feasible given the limitations (time, cost, staff, effort) of the project?

- Does the report show any shortcomings in the systems as it stands, e.g. potential security weakness?

- Are the recommendations comprehensive, showing the implications for the rest of the system and the effect on performance, security, etc?

- Does the analysis conform to the limitations and standards set for the exercise?

- If any shortcomings have been reported, does the analysis recommend further steps which can be taken?

- Does the report provide enough information to make a sound decision as to what should be done with the model now?

Data management specification

The data structures proposed in this specification should be inspected by those with expertise in data management as well as members of the project team. Hitherto, the data structures existed as concepts: now those who are going to convert them into reality must see that they conform to their standards and take another look at the technical feasibility of the data structures. Although data management experts should have been involved in the review of the system specification and, ideally, in the design of the data structures as well, they will now have another chance to evaluate them before acting on them. It is also possible that changes might have crept in after the system specification was complete.

- Do the proposed structures comply with company standards, e.g. naming conventions?

- Do they derive entirely from the system specification?

- When compared with the system specification, are there any omissions, alterations or deletions?

- Are the descriptions concise, accurate and unambiguous?

- Is there any conflict between the proposed structures and items and the technical capabilities of the physical data structures?

- Is the method of optimising the data structures really going to be effective?

- Can performance criteria really be met?

- Could the new structures cause any security risks if implemented as they stand?

- Is there any potential redundancy, for example, when compared with existing structures?

- Is there anything in the document which needs to be tested for feasibility before acceptance?

- Is the type of data structure familiar? If not, are there any implications for data management staff, for example training?

- Does the document specify that test structures are needed? If so, are there any problems?

- Is there a provisional date for implementing the new structure? If so, is it reasonable? Are there any implications for existing structures and processing? Normally, this will be included in the implementation plan but early warning will be appreciated.

- Is a package going to be implemented? If so, the above questions should also be asked about its data.

End of phase

The System Specification phase ends when the following activities have been completed.

- The system specification has been finished and accepted as the basis of the new system.

- Data structures defined in the system specification have been accepted by whoever is responsible for data management.

- If an applications package is being used, the evaluation has been completed.

- If a prototype has been used, the model has been analysed and either incorporated into the system in some way or else rejected.

In this phase, the separate strands of package evaluation and prototype analysis are brought together. With the project team's system specification as the detailed description of the system as a whole, supported by package documentation, the work of converting the system from logical concept into physical reality can now begin in earnest. The data management specification was the first step and the next phase will concentrate mainly on processing.

5 Programming and testing

During this phase, the system is transformed from concept to reality. Programmers are now key members of the project team, whereas they have not been involved at all until now, except for consultation. Therefore, one of the first things the project manager should do is to introduce them to the project and to the new system, showing what contribution to the business it will make. Of course, some programmers may be happy enough to write programs without any idea of what the system will do but others find it galling not to be involved. In any case, programmers are often involved in system tests and an understanding of the business function of the system will make it easier to understand why some processes are linked. Certainly anyone who has any contact with the user ought to have a basic understanding of the system's business role.

Unless a package is being used for some of the processing, the source of all activity during this phase is the completed detailed system specification and supporting design documentation. It must be possible to trace all processing described in the program specifications back to this documentation. Naturally, each program must do no less and no more than its specification requires. The system test, too, must follow a plan which is based entirely on the data and processing described in the system specification.

Control of documentation and organising activity can be quite difficult. During each of the last two phases, we concentrated on a single key document – the system proposal and the detailed system specification. Now the content of the latter document is divided into a number of program specifications which in turn become programs. Together with other system components such as job streams, they then have to be re-assembled into the system (see Figure 5.1).

Unless documentation is tightly controlled now, it is easy to end up with a program which does not do what the latest version of its specification requires or to miss an important linked test. This is especially true if the system specification has to be changed for any reason. It will be necessary to laboriously trace the change through to each program specification and program. Depending on how much work has been carried out, program designs, program coding, program test plans and the system test plan will all have to be re-examined and possibly altered and tested again. Such modifications should only be required if, for example, some major external factor such as a change in law makes it obligatory to alter the system quite drastically. Can there be a better reason for asking the user to agree, before this phase begins, that the system will not be changed until after implementation?

If an applications package is to be part of the system, it should be ready for integrated testing. The package should have been selected during the previous phase and should be installed and available by the time it is required. The evaluation should have tested the package *per se*: now we have to see that it works with the rest of the system.

109

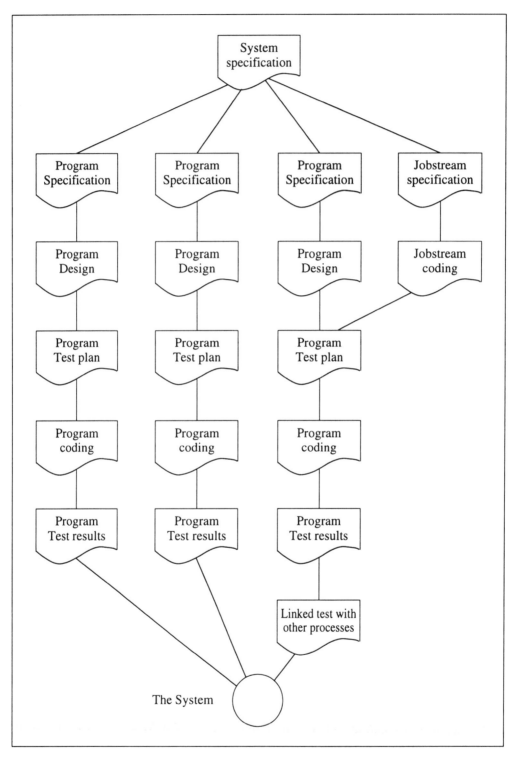

Figure 5.1   Components of the System

If a prototype was used, it is time to make sure that the exercise has been brought to an end. Indeed, most prototypes should have served their purpose before or during the previous phase. If, for example, the aim of the prototype was to help clarify the system's functionality, it should have fulfilled its purpose during the Definition phase. If the prototype was a scaled-down version of the full system, the project manager should have decided how to convert it and used it as a basis for the system specification during the last phase. Perhaps the prototype was built in order to find an acceptable method of screen-handling. In that case, the method should be available for the system test.

A good project plan will bring all these activities together showing which depend on others, as well as providing the means of putting resources where they are needed. It should also be flexible enough to allow changes to be made. The number of computer people involved in the project is at its maximum during this phase. The project manager will find life easier if some work is delegated, for example control of all programming might be given to a programming manager, especially on a large project. Care should be taken to ensure that the reporting lines and channels of communication are clear and that the programming manager cannot be bypassed. Who has not come across second rate systems analysts who seek to divert attention from shortcomings in their specifications by asking programmers to make a few quick changes as a favour?

Review is as important during this phase as any other. It is normally easier to trace things back to a source document now, especially when programming begins since everything in a program design or in its coding must be derived from the program specification. The earliest formal software inspections were of program coding and their benefits are well-known through Michael Fagan's writings. Whatever the pressure on the project team, review should not be abandoned just because programs are tested. Testing does not show everything and it is not worth jeopardising the success of a system because an important program is inefficient or difficult to maintain.

Phase initiation

The phase begins when the system specification, including processing and data structures has been completed and accepted by all interested parties, especially the users and computer centre management. If an applications package is being used, the selection must have been made and it should be installed for testing by the time the first system test is planned.

If prototyping is being used, it should have been completed by now unless it only concerns screen handling,etc. This must be ready by the time the system test begins.

Documents

Most of the documents are of interest only to the project team now. Do not forget, however, that some will be read by future generations of systems development staff who will not have been involved in the project. Always think of program specifications, designs and coding as being meant for people who will have to be guided entirely by the document to find out what a program does.

- Revised project plan
  - Target audience: project team;

    users;

    computer department management .

- Program specification
  - Target audience: project team.
- Other processing specification
  - Target audience: project team.
- Program design
  - Target audience: project team.
- Program coding
  - Target audience: project team.
- Program test plan
  - Target audience: project team.
- Program test results
  - Target audience: project team.
- Testing other processing
  - Target audience: project team.
- System test plan
  - Target audience: project team.
- System test results
  - Target audience: project team;

    users.

Project plan

Revision of the project plan as a whole

- Were the estimates for the previous phase correct?
- Is any modification to the estimates for the remainder of the project necessary in consequence?
- Has any possible delay in completion been identified? If so, is it likely to cause any problems for the users?
- Is any work from the previous phase not yet complete? If so, how will this affect the current phase?

Detailed planning of the current phase

There are almost certainly going to be more activities during this phase than any others. Although most only involve the project team, on a large project this may now have expanded greatly with additional teams of programmers responsible for different parts of the system. In addition, work on integrating a package may be required.

If management is delegated, it should be done in a fairly formal way. A subset of the plan should identify which parts of the system are being dealt with by which staff. On the surface this is easy enough, but reality is rarely so simple. For example, a project manager might decide that a system falls quite neatly into three parts, say input, processing and output. A programming team, supervised by a chief programmer, could be made responsible for each of these parts. The project manager appoints systems analysts to write program specifications for each of the three parts and, so long as the programming managers do their work, what could be easier?

In practice, a lot can go wrong with this approach, both from a technical and a managerial point of view. How will the different parts of the system interface? Input and output programs may both interface with other systems and some parts of the system may use common processing, will this be done in a consistent way? If one programming team depends on another one for something to be done, how will this be monitored? What will happen if one programming team decides data has to be changed slightly, to make processing easier, and goes ahead? If one team finishes their programs while another is falling behind, how can we re-allocate resources?

The point is that the more you delegate the easier it is to let controls slip. The best safeguards against this risk are planning, consistency and communications. Each of the programming managers should have a detailed plan which is not merely a means of supervision. It is an integral part of the project plan with channels of communication laid down, procedures for dealing with areas of common interest such as interfaces. Standards and working methods should also be identical within each programming team. It should be possible to transfer any programmer from one part of the system to another without having to learn a new way of working.

Therefore, the detailed planning for the project should address these problems and not merely farm out the programming. If everyone is working to the same type of plan, the phase will be much more easy to control. A thorough review of the plan, preferably involving key systems and programming staff, will also be beneficial in pointing out possible problem areas.

The following checklist gives guidance in planning for all activities related to programming. The project manager may well delegate some parts of it, indeed this is most likely on large projects. In that case, it will be necessary to make sure that the delegated parts are all written to the same standard.

- How will the system be divided up for programming purposes?

- Who will be involved in the programming? Note the role and responsibilities of each person, particularly those with supervisory duties.

- What standards apply to the specifications, including version control, presentation and naming conventions?

- What standards apply to programming? These should include version control, documentation, naming conventions and presentation of test results.

- Which programming languages are going to be used?

- Are all staff fully conversant with the output of the methodology used? Will they have to consult the output of the previous phase or will methodology diagrams be used in the program specifications?

- Is training required? If so, when can it be arranged?
- To what extent will staff be interchangeable, i.e. able to work on additional programs if necessary?
- Which programs are dependent on others? Which programs need to be tested together?
- Which programs need to be specified and written first?
- Which processes will be shared by groups of programmers e.g. in testing?
- When will staff need to cooperate, for example:
  - defining interfaces;
  - testing common processes;
  - making changes?
- What are the rules for making changes, for example, who can authorise them and how will changes be communicated to the rest of the project team?
- How will each of the documents produced be reviewed?
- What review methods will be used?
- Which programs will be reviewed and how? Consider those which have some special requirement such as great speed and efficiency and those which are very complex. If a program interfaces with others, it is advisable that the specification and coding should be reviewed by at least some of those responsible for the other programs.
- Which other processes need to be specified and tested?
- Who will be responsible for creating and maintaining test data? Shared test data needs to be controlled. It is also useful to have a common pool of test data which can be accessed by all for their own testing – so long as they make sure that everything in the test plan is tested.
- What are the tasks for this phase? The production of each of the documents listed above should be treated as a task even if it is performed by the same person.
- How much time is to be allocated for each task?
- When will each task begin and end?
- What tasks other than programming have to be done? Who will perform then and what time will be allocated for them?
- If a prototype is going to be integrated into the system:
  - who will be responsible;
  - what are the timescales;
  - how will it be tested?
- If a package is going to be integrated into the system:
  - who will be responsible;
    - what are the timescales;
    - how will it be tested?

When planning for systems testing consider the following.

- Who is responsible for the plan?

- How long will it take to write the plan?

- Who will review the plan?

- Who will take part in the test?

- Who will be responsible for creating the test data?

- Who other than the project team be involved in the test, e.g. operations staff and users? when will they be available?

- When will the testing of each process begin and end?

- How much time and what resources will be allocated to each test?

Program specification

Every program specification has two functions: the first is to tell the programmer what the program should do; the second is to inform any reader what the program actually does. The specification must therefore be kept up to date at all times, throughout the life of the program.

Both of these categories of readers are important. The goal of the author of a program specification should be to communicate the way the program functions to any future reader, not merely the first. It is wrong to think that a program specification is primarily about the first time the program is written. Most programs are amended, sometimes frequently.

Needless to say, it should be possible to trace all of the processing in the program specification back to the systems specification.

A good program specification should never tell the programmer how to write programs. For a good programmer, to be told that the program should make use of such and such programming commands by a systems analyst is to be patronised. Even if the systems analyst was once a good programmer, experience is quickly forgotten and improved techniques will soon make the former programmer's knowledge outdated. An inexperienced programmer can receive plenty of good advice from the programming manager or a senior colleague who will see that the specification is converted first into a design and then into a program.

That is not to say that a systems analyst should not be aware of the capabilities of a programming language. This is particularly true of a high-level language or a Fourth Generation language where choice regarding processing may be limited by the way the language actually works. For example, databases have a means of locking either a data item, a record or even a file so that access by others is restricted. There is no point in the author of a program specification stating that a certain means of locking is required when it is known that the program will be written in a language that does not permit the kind of locking the analyst has in mind. If it becomes clear that the computer department's selection of computer languages will not permit the system to be written, that is another matter – one to be referred to management .

The specification should explain what processing has to be carried out as clearly as possible without recourse to any jargon, especially the jargon of the user department. Programmers, who may have just been brought into the project during this phase, should not be expected to have an indepth knowledge of the business area for which the system is intended and may easily misunderstand if subjected to too much unfamiliar terminology.

The author of a program specification should seek the advice of the programming manager about the presentation and language to be used unless guidelines or standards are already in place. A good specification should explain processes in clear, logical terms and should therefore include diagrams, mathematical formulae and decision tables where necessary. There is also no reason why structured phraseology should not be used even if it breaks the rules of natural language syntax. It may be easier to follow the argument in this way.

Structured phraseology is essentially a method of writing logic. Conventions may differ but should not deviate too far from Boolean logic. Indeed, this kind of phraseology is at its best when used to explain logical requirements. Below is a simple example. The conventions here are that names in lower case stand for local storage (i.e. within the program only) and those in upper case refer to standard names used on a permanent file.

If result-of-calculation > 0 then

1. update matching SALES-FILE as follows:

    move SALES-COST to OLD-SALES-COST

    move calculated-value to SALES-COST

2. add SALES-COST to running sales-cost-total

3. add "1" to valid-recs-processed.

The example assumes that two matching records have already been found and that this fact has been explained previously.

The layout of a program specification will be dictated by departmental standards. Some standards prescribe a format in minute detail but do not always ensure that the function of the program and its history can easily be traced from the specification. The first page of the specification should include the items given below as a minimum.

The identity of the program within the system. This is normally a code, e.g. PA-002. This might be a program in the pension accounts system.

The original author of the specification.

Version number.

The date the original version was written.

The author, date and version number of each amendment and a concise description of the changes. A record should be kept whenever any amendment is made, even before the program is released for live running. You may wish to use a different method of version control before and after implementation. See Appendix 2 – Managing Change.

A brief introduction of the program's function.

A contents page, unless the specification is very small.

The contents, too, will be subject to departmental standards. Consideration should be given to the following.

Associated programs and processing

- What programs, subprograms or other processes such as streamed jobs are associated with this one? This should include any linked processing such as programs triggered off by this one.

- How does this one depend on them?

- How do the others depend on this one?

- How are they linked, i.e. what event determines that one calls the other?

- If this program is called by another (e.g. a subprogram) what parameters does it expect and what should it send back to the calling program?

- If this program calls another program what parameters should it send and what will be returned from the other program – including error messages?

Data

The term 'file' may indicate any sort of file including a database structure.

- What files are accessed by this program?

- How are they accessed by this program, i.e. read, updated, created or deleted?

- What external files are accessed by this program, including files belonging to other systems, other sites, other companies?

- How are files accessed, i.e. what keys or parameters are needed?

- What is the procedure for accessing files, e.g. through other files or by a network?

- What is the format of each file?

- What data items are needed? Where are the data items held (refer to the files)?

- How are they accessed?

- What format s are used?

- What permitted values are attributed to them? This may be a function of the database management system.

The specification should include a layout of all files and the data items within the file. Report layouts and input screen layouts are also needed. Sometimes the same data item may occur in more than one file. If so, it must be qualified. The specification should make clear if any item has a particular, technical function. For example, a database file will normally have one or more items which can be used as keys to access it rapidly. A file may be sorted in a particular sequence using one or more of its data items. This sort of information must be conveyed to the programmer.

The specification should use the technical name of the data, i.e. the file and data item names which may be held on a dictionary. The letter should provide a good description, including precise details of formats and permitted values. If so, it can be used as a source for the program specification. By all means, extract what is needed for the program specification from the dictionary but do not state in the specification that details of the data structures can be obtained from the dictionary and leave it to the programmer to find out what they are. It may be convenient but what if the data structures change? If any modification is made to them, the program may be affected and that means that the specification will be affected as well. The specification describes the situation on the date it is written. Any change to the data used in the program warrants a revised specification.

Definitions of structures such as files should include:

- anticipated volumes;
- changes to size after processing;
- sequence of records;
- means of access.

Definitions of data items should include:

- format (e.g. ASCII, EBCDIC);
- size, number of decimal places;
- maximum and minimum potential value;
- permitted values;
- base values.

Processing

This describes everything the program actually does, mainly the way it handles the data. It is helpful if the logic of processing is described chronologically i.e. what happens first should come first. Avoid back referencing if possible. If the program does not follow the same sequence as the specification, it will only be because of the constraints of the language. The only variation on this is if common processing is used in different parts of the program. Clearly, it should only be described in one place. If you need to specify common processing, simply give it a name such as a paragraph reference and, whenever it is needed, state that this processing needs to be invoked. All details such as parameters should be given in the description of the common processing.

The following checklist should be used when considering the contents.

- How is each data structure accessed? Consider:
  - how is the key or parameter used to access the file derived;
  - what other actions have to be provided e.g. specifying an access mode;
  - what indicates success or failure;
  - what has to be done if success or failure is indicated?
- What validation is needed, for example:
  - comparison with another file;
  - range checks;
  - permitted values?

- What screens are used by the system?
- What is the function of each screen?
- What process invokes the screen?
- What processes are controlled by the screen?
- How are screens initialised? Consider:
  - how is access to the screen permitted and how is the permission given;
  - what base values are assigned to a screen when it is first presented to the user;
  - how might the contents of the screen vary for different classes of users;
  - what needs to be done to allow the user to invoke the screen handling procedures such as function keys?
- What calculations are required?
- When and how are they invoked?
- What is done at every step in each calculation? A worked example can be useful when explaining complex calculations.
- What intermediate results are there? How are they used?
- What rounding is required at each stage? Do not forget assumed decimal points.
- How are files modified by this program?
- What estimated volumes of data will be read from or written to each file?
- When precisely does output have to be produced? Can it be deferred?
- What is the sequence of output?
- For printed output what special stationery is needed?
- What communication with computer operations is required? In particular, what operator intervention is needed and how will the operator be informed what to do and when to do it?
- What event starts the program and what determines that it is finished?
- How is successful completion indicated?

Errors and exceptions

The error messages given out by applications software may be adequate for computer personnel but will probably just confuse users, unless they are supplemented by something more intelligible. Therefore, any error messages seen by users should tell them what to do, in terms they can understand, even if it is only to inform the computer centre and quote an error condition.

The programmer also needs to know what has to be done when any exception or error is encountered. Here are some examples.

- What should be done if data cannot be accessed for any reason?

- What should be done if an error condition is present? Consider:

  - content of the error messages (is the standard message enough?);
  - instructions to computer operators;
  - what to do with a transaction which has started but has not yet been completed;
  - what should be done with transactions which have been completed but which may need modification;
  - what effect the condition will have on the rest of the system;
  - how should information about the problem be communicated to the rest of the system.

Standard error messages should be supplemented by enough details to enable corrections to be made or, if that is not possible, to permit the rapid discovery of the cause of the problem.

Security and controls

- What security requirements are a feature of the system and how do they affect this program?
- At what precise points should controls be placed, bearing in mind the importance of the control being independent of whatever process it is validating?
- What should be done if there is any breach of security, including availability and integrity?

Hardware requirements

- With what hardware does the program interface? This might include local printers or networks. If processing is affected by this, the specification should provide the following details:

  - how the hardware is accessed;
  - how successful access is indicated;
  - what should be done about any situation in which the interface cannot be used.

Other processing specification

In all systems there are a number of processes which have to be defined and specified but which cannot be classified as programs. The most obvious example is that of the job stream, which may run an entire suite of programs. Another example is the menu system which the user first sees when logging on to the computer. It may give access to processing in addition to those specified for the system, for example electronic mail, word processing and spreadsheets. Such software is now widely used and may already be available to all users of the new system. They will want to be able to choose between accessing these processes or the new system.

If the system is a database system, the users will probably want to be able to extract data from the system, either for their own reporting or to copy data to other applications packages. Accountants often use spreadsheets to analyse financial data extracted from a database. The ability to do this should have been specified as a requirement of the system but the best way of satisfying it may not be a program. A good end-user reporting package should provide facilities for data extraction. If such a package is available, all the project manager has to do is to see that its facilities can be accessed by the users; that they work properly and that the users knows what to do. Otherwise a rather complex program may have to be specified.

How should you deal with these processes? The project manager will see that the detailed system specification is broken down into a number of programs. It is merely a question of identifying what else needs to be done so that no feature of the system is omitted. What processes cannot be dealt with by writing program specifications? What needs to be done to make the processes work together?

There will probably be a number of job streams which can be specified, tested and handed over much as a program but without the need for designing it first. If end-user reporting is a requirement for the new system, it should be treated as part of the system and tested before the system is handed over. This means thinking about how it fits in with the users' work, how it is going to be controlled and so on. The checklist given below on end-user reporting should provide enough information. If it is necessary to integrate the system with other applications via a menu, this should also be the subject of a specification. In practice, this may mean very little work if standard menus are used.

Therefore, the project manager will have to decide where the process will be part of a program specification and where another form of specification might be appropriate (*see* Figure 5.2). So long as all processing is specified, tested and documented as necessary, the user should have all features of the system available from the day of implementation.

To recap, then, the project manager should consider:

- Should this process something which we can best perform without writing an applications program specification?

- What is the best way of performing this process?

- What needs to be done to specify it, test it and document it? Standards will make this easier.

- Does the documentation need to be part of the permanent documentation of the system, i.e. updated whenever modified?

Whatever is specified should be subject to the normal rules of documentation for computer systems, i.e. with a clear reference number (e.g. a job number or suite number), an author, date and version.

Checklists for the three processes discussed above, namely job streams, end-user reporting and menus are given below.

Job streams

The following checklist should be used when writing specifications for job streams.

- What is the title of the job?

- What files does it access?

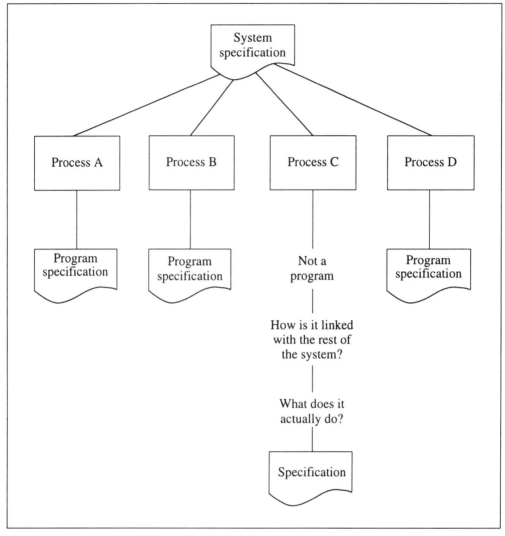

Figure 5.2   Other forms of processing

- How are the files accessed, e.g. access mode?
- What processes does it control (e.g. applications programs?
- What should be done with the output? Make it clear if it can or should be deferred.
- What special stationery is needed?
- What communication with the programs is needed? At the very least, a program should indicate if it has finished correctly or if an error condition has been encountered. Any messages from the program should also be picked up and displayed.
- What messages for the operator will be generated?
- What should the operator do if the job finishes correctly?
- What should the operator do if an error occurs?

- What volumes are anticipated and what will be the effect on file sizes?

- When will the job be run?

- What documentation is needed? Most computer departments will have standards for documenting job streams, including at least the name of the author, version number, the date it was written, a brief description and the amendment history. The author of the specification may decide that additional information will be useful, for example if the programs require parameters. A list of files and the way they are accessed within the programs is also useful, although it should be available from the operational documentation.

- How can this job be tested? It may be possible to combine it with a program test – so long as this is planned and the results recorded. If it runs a number of programs or is linked with other processes special testing may be needed.

End-user reporting

Assuming that the system is going to have end-user reporting as a facility, how should this be incorporated? The package will have already been evaluated and tested to see whether it works. The problem is to make it work for the users so that it becomes a useful, integral part of the system.

There is normally a manager function for a package which allows access rights to be determined. Whether or not this is eventually controlled by a user or by the computer department will depend on local practice. The project team will have to first set up the system and this will be much easier if it is thought of as a process to be specified. A specification should consider the following points.

- Which categories of user should have access to end user reporting?

- What access rights will each have?

- How will access rights be controlled?

- What will each user be allowed to do with the data? Some may be allowed to copy data to a personal computer while others might be restricted to reading data only.

- How will the end-user reporting be accessed? Will this be from one menu or several?

- Is a data dictionary part of the package? If so what modification is needed so that it will suit our requirements?

- If no dictionary is available, how will the users understand what data is available, what names they should user, etc?

- What needs to be set up so that the users can make full use of the facilities the package offers? This might include local storage areas and files, the means of copying data and so on.

Menus

Menus are the most frequently used part of an on-line system. A well-designed menu system, will allow users to move conveniently from process to process. It should mirror normal working patterns as far as possible.

Writing menu systems as a series of programs is tedious; nowadays they are normally packaged. Therefore, the specification will have to take into account the restrictions of the chosen menu system while trying to make it as easy to use as possible. The following checklist should be considered.

- What processes are going to be used by each category of user? Consider the sequence of normal working.

- In what circumstances will users need to leave one process, perform a task and then return? For example, it might be necessary to update a master file record or copy data from elsewhere while performing a transaction.

- Apart from the functions of the system under development, what other facilities will be provided from the menus, e.g. electronic mail? What methods of reaching these facilities will be most convenient to the users?

- How will users be able to reach key parts of the system or to exit from a process quickly?

- How will they access on-line 'help'?

- What function keys will be used? Standard labelling and functionality is needed if the users are not going to be utterly confused. It should be as consistent as possible with the labelling and functionality of the screens generated by the system.

Program design

A program should be designed before coding begins. It is far easier to trap major errors and to uncover inefficiency by reviewing a design, than it is by wading through reams of coding. In the long run, you will save time and effort by doing so. The more complex a program is, the more important it is to design it. There are a number of design methods and the programming manager should make sure that a suitable one is used.

The aim of the design is to show how the program can best be written – but what constitutes the best way? Should the emphasis be on speed of processing or maintainability? Also, what level of detail is required? The programming manager will provide specific guidance but, in general, you should aim to produce a program which is easy to maintain from a design which shows the structure of the program, paths, processes, calls to other processes and all input and output.

The checklist given below will obviously be supplemented by local standards. Some questions deal with problems which might arise from the specification and these should have been trapped when the specification was reviewed. They are included here because the person designing the program will be looking at it in great detail and might come across something which escaped notice.

Also, practice can vary widely about some matters such as error processing. Should the specification lay down what should happen if data accessed by the program is not perfect? How will the program trap such an error? It may be assumed that a file will always be available – what if someone has opened it exclusively for some reason?

There may also be error conditions which indicate a software fault which is not directly attributable to the processing contained within the program, in other words a 'bug' in the manufacturer's software. For example it may be impossible to read data because the internal linkage of a database management system has been corrupted. The programming manager is likely to know about the current bugs and to have found ways of avoiding them. Therefore, whatever standard way of dealing with such problems the program manager has developed will need to be catered for in the design.

- Is there any part of the specification which is unclear or ambiguous? If so, it must be altered.

- What is the sequence of processing? How can the design simulate it?

- Is there any part of the specification which cannot be included in the design, for example if it will need to be written in a different language? Perhaps this can be dealt with by writing a subprogram called from this one but, at all events, the specification should probably be altered.

- Does the specification make any assumptions about the data which might not be true? For example, it might assume that data output from another process is going to be valid. What will happen if the data was corrupted before it was accessed by this program?

- Can any processes be combined, even though defined separately? Sometimes a program specification will not identify common processing shared by a number of other processes and it may be more efficient to create a subroutine? Against this you should ask yourself – which way will be most easy to maintain?

- What should be done if data or files are unobtainable?

- Are there any possible error conditions which will be dealt with by normal programming practice? What is their significance for the program?

- What processes control other processes? How do they communicate?

- Are there any requirements for great efficiency, for example speed of access, or complex processing to deal with some technical problem? Otherwise, the program should be designed with ease of maintenance in mind.

- What relationship does this program have with others? Does it call other programs or is it called by other programs?

- Are there any internal controls, for example record counts? How can the design ensure that they will be independent of the process they are controlling when the program is written?

Program coding

Standards are widely used for program coding. Many are specific to a particular language. Here we are only concerned with making the program coding easy to understand. Naturally, the program should follow the structure of the design.

- What is needed to identify this program in future? The minimum data needed here are program number, date and author, version number and a brief description of the function. There should also be an amendment history updated whenever any change is subsequently made.

- What does each function actually do? A description of each section should enable a reader to trace it back both to the program specification and to the design.

- Is this processing complex or is it completely obvious what is happening? Any complex processing should be explained. Bear in mind that the next person to look at the listing may have very little idea what the system does.

- Are parameters used? Their names, sizes, formats and permitted values should be documented.

- What local storage is needed? Give a description of the names, saying how it is used by the program. If local storage has some special significance such as an indicator, give the possible values and meaning.

- Is there a better way of proceeding than is laid down in the design? If so, the programming manager should be consulted but the design should be followed unless the design is also changed.

Program test plan

Programs should be tested to prove that they work according to the specification and design. A test plan for a program will make this easier and also provide something which can be used to verify the results.

The plan should state what is being tested, how it is being tested and what the results should be. It should also be possible to trace each test back to the program specification by a paragraph or section reference. If you enter the results of each test on the same document it will eventually become a record of the tests. See below under 'Program test results'.

Program testing is a difficult area because there may be millions of paths through even a simple program. How much can you reasonably be expected to test? There is no simple answer and no substitute for the guidance of an experienced programming manager. In general, it is reasonable to say that you can make a distinction between the function of programs in terms of what would happen if something went wrong. In other words, you conduct a kind of impact analysis.

Take for example a program which is an important part of an aircraft traffic control system or one used in analysing medical data for patients with serious heart conditions. The consequences of a mistake could be catastrophic and would justify extremely rigorous, time-consuming testing of all programs and the system as a whole.

In most cases, the potential for damage is less serious. By planning the testing so it is comprehensive, testing all processes, but concentrating on the most critical and difficult parts of the program, you will be most likely to test the program thoroughly. Test plans which put a lot of data through the 'easy bits' of a program are of no use. One rule of thumb is to think of 80% of all paths as a rough guide. If the test plan covers less than 80% of all paths, is it going to be enough in view of everything we know about the program's future role? It may be that you decide that 80% is much too high but at least you have thought about it.

This checklist covers a number of general points regarding testing and not all will be applicable to every program.

- What is the overall function of the program in terms of input, processing and output?

- What possible paths can be taken when the program is run? The tests should prove the following:

  - error handling;

- optional paths however they are selected, e.g. by user choice or by program logic;
- parameters.

- What are the discrete processes within the specification?
- How can each be tested and how does it relate to others?
- What do we need to do to prove a calculation really works, showing intermediate as well as final results if necessary?
- What validation of data is present? Consider what will happen if:
  - no data is present;
  - data falls outside the permitted value, for the type of validation, for example, exceeding the maximum or minimum possible values for a number.
- What will happen if data is corrupted in some way and this is not trapped by validation? Could an output file be corrupted?
- What will happen if volumes of data exceed those anticipated?
- What will happen if data needed by the program is unavailable, e.g. if a file cannot be accessed?
- When data is output, what happens if permitted ranges are exceeded?
- Does this program depend on others? If so, what happens if one of these programs is not run?
- What happens if this program is accidentally run twice?
- What performance requirements are there? How will they be tested?
- What happens if a subprogram called by this one is unavailable?
- If the program reads a number of record, and copies them into its own internal storage, what happens if more records are present than expected and all are copied?
- Can internal data areas be overwritten by more than one process? What will happen if indicators set by one process are overwritten by another?
- What data is available for testing this program? Note the origins.
- What additional data is needed?
- Is the program normally run as part of a job? If so, can the job be tested here? Error conditions and paths in the job control language must be tested as well.

Program test results

A good test plan will make the preparation of test results easier. They should be presented in such a way that anyone reviewing them can see what tests have been carried out and what the results are.

For an online system, the easiest way of checking test results is to look at a screen. Providing written evidence of numerous tests in the form of hard copies of screens can be very time-consuming. However, this should not be used as an excuse for not presenting test results. The test plan should state what the anticipated results were so all the person testing the program needs to do is to record that these results were indeed obtained. An additional step is to demonstrate the tests to someone else and have the results verified in that way.

As for presentation, if the test plan has been well documented, it is best to follow it as closely as possible. Indeed, it may be easy to use the same word processing document and alter it to show the tests have been carried out.

The following brief checklist assumes that a test plan has been drawn up and the only concerns are presentation and certification of results.

- Is it advisable to have the results certified by someone else? This should be considered if test results are difficult to interpret or if hard copies are unavailable.

- If it is difficult to include test results as evidence, how can the test be guaranteed? As well as certification by another person, could the test be easily reproduced?

- What are the results? How can they best be presented? There may be several stages to a test and the links between them should be shown, together with intermediate result.

- How do the results prove the test has worked?

- Are printed reports available? If so, what additional information is needed to show that they prove a test has worked?

- Who has carried out the tests? The results of each should be signed by the person carrying out the test, together with the date.

Testing other processing

Under 'Other processing specification', we looked at three types of processing which cannot be described as programming and ask – how can we test them? A simple test plan and set of results like those used for program testing should be the goal .

Job streams

In the case of job streams the answer is often quite simple: it can be combined with the program test. This possibility has been mentioned above and, so long as the testing is planned and documented, it should be adequate. Matters become more complex when a number of programs are combined in one job, especially if some are only run when certain conditions are met.

For example, the first program in a job stream may run successfully or fail. If it is successful the next program will run. If it fails, the remaining programs might be skipped and a special program run to restore the database to the condition it was in before the error occurred. All this will be controlled by the job control language and this can become quite complex. So, its logic will need to be properly tested. The same applies to separate job streams which depend on one another – the conditions for one following the other also need to be tested.

Leaving such linked testing to the system test may mean that an error of logic goes undetected. Even if system testing does uncover such errors, it is not the best time to be making quick changes to complex logic. The best course is to require linked testing where necessary. Since we are dealing with logic, the test plan and results will be very similar to those for program testing (notably the testing of paths through a program) and the same checklists can be used eclectically. This checklist provides some pointers to deciding what the linked testing should look for.

- Can this job stream be tested a part of the program testing? This should normally be done when the job stream runs a single program?

- What are the paths within this job stream? What determines that it follows a certain logical path?

- What are the results of each program and how does one depend on the other?

- What happens when one program terminates in error? Do all the recovery procedures and error flags work properly?

- What triggers off this job stream? If it is another job, what will happen if the first job fails?

- What subsequent jobs depend on this one? How does this job communicate with the next?

- What happens to the data if this or any related job fails?

End-user reporting

If you have written your own programs to do this, they should be tested like any others. In most cases, a package will be used and the testing should be to set up the functions for a number of users to make sure that it can access the data and files it is supposed to access. If there are different categories of users, ensure that a representative sample of each is available, especially if some have supervisory functions such as permitting access rights.

You should not now be concerned with proving that the package works – that should have been done when it was evaluated. At most you should consider the points in the checklist for specifying end-user reporting and ask yourself – is this something which needs to be tested? Look at it from the point of view of a user in terms of understanding what can be done with the data.

- Will a user recognise what data is available? Will the names used mean anything?

- Can the end-user reporting easily be accessed?

- How will the user extract data?

- Will it be apparent what the user can do with the data? If it is copied for another process, for example, as input to a spreadsheet, what has to be done when the file has been created?

- If a user supervisor is empowered to give other users access rights, is the procedure clear and secure?

Beyond this, the system test and user acceptance testing should prove adequate.

Menus

The menu system may have been developed via a prototype or belong to a menu package. The latter may be part of a screen handling Fourth Generation programming language which gives the users input screens. If so, menus have to be tested as an integral part of program testing. Beyond that the testing should concentrate on the main functions given in the checklist for specifying menus. Consider also the following.

- Does the menu give access to the processes it is supposed to?

- What happens if one of the processes fails?

- If you have the option of leaving one screen temporarily in order to access another, can you always get back again? What happens to the data on the first screen if the called screen fails?

- Can you exit properly?

- Do linked processes, which are not part of the system being developed, work properly?

- Do the function keys do what they say they will?

Further testing will be carried out during the system testing and user acceptance testing.

System test plan

The object of the system test is to prove that every function of the system works correctly. This means not only that everything in the system specification must be tested, but also everything the users will be doing even if not defined as programs. If the system has end-user reporting, if it is linked to another system or package or if it is accessed remotely by some users – all such features should be tested.

A system test should not reproduce the detailed low-level testing suitable for proving that an individual program does everything the program specification says it should. It should concentrate on showing that the system as a whole functions as it is specified and as it will be used when implemented. This means that testing will reproduce day-today running, month-end processing with a view to showing that the system works as a number of integrated items of software and as a means to a business end.

However, as in the case of program testing, one of the concerns of the project manager will be to ensure that testing is sufficient for the criticality of the system. The potential damage of any failure is greater for some systems than others .

- How many complete tests of the entire system will be needed? In what respects will they differ if at all? A problem-free final run is convincing evidence of thoroughness.

- What are the individual processes which will be tested? Each should represent a single activity, identified by a suitable title such as 'profit centre reporting' or 'pension calculation'.

- How should these single activities be combined as a test module, a group of related tests, e.g. 'profit centre month-end processing' or 'pension record maintenance'?

- Who will carry out each test?

- How will the test data be generated? If data is going to be copied from another environment, how will it be modified?

- If data used for testing is derived from a live environment, what security measures will be needed to keep it confidential? Do not forget that with data protection laws it is illegal to use data about living people for testings.

- When will each test be performed?

- Who will certify the test results as correct?

- What user involvement will there be? Their assistance on menu handling and end-user reporting during this stage will be timely.

- When will the programs, jobs, etc., which will be used to test each module, be ready?

- What are the criteria which will prove that each of the processes or modules being tested are indeed correct? The following information should be recorded.

  - the name and aim of each individual test;

  - the programs, job streams, etc. which will be used in the test;

  - the data which will be used, including any parameters;

  - the anticipated results, including intermediate results.

  As well as showing that valid data is processed correctly, the tests should prove that invalid data is rejected and shown to be rejected.

- How will access of data from remote sites be tested?

- Which tests receive data from, or transmit data to, other systems?

- How will the results be presented?

- What provision is there for testing recovery in the event of any problem occurring, such as data corruption, system malfunction and so on?

- What provision is there for testing speed of response and speed of processing?

- How will potential minimum and maximum volumes of data be tested?

System test results

The system test results should follow the system test plan closely. The same word processing document can be taken and modified. The results should be certified by whoever is responsible for the system test as a whole.

If it has been agreed that the results should be presented to the users, a summary together with copies of screens and examples of reports may be the best method. The full results, supplemented as they may be by reams of reports and so on, may be excessive. At the very least, however, a user summary should mention all the processes which have been tested and give the results of performance tests to show that a satisfactory level has been achieved. For performance tests, it is worth considering a graphical representation, perhaps showing the effect of processing peaks.

The checklist for program test results can be used here, as well.

Review

Program specification

The review of the program specification should involve at least one person with good technical knowledge of programming and the capabilities of the programming language being used.

- Can a programmer design and write a good program using this specification?
- Can the processes the specification describes be converted into code? If a language has already been designated by the programming manager, consider the capabilities of that particular language.
- How will the anticipated volumes of data affect the processing?
- Are requirements for speed of processing, etc., realistic? If not, what can be done to achieve them?
- Have the data structures been authorised and do they already exist as a test version?
- Is it clear precisely what data structures are needed, how they are accessed and the format, size and base and permitted values of all of the data?
- Do the contents conform to the project standards?
- Is the program derived from a discrete process described in the system specification?
- Is there anything in the specification which cannot be traced back to the system specification?
- Is there anything in the relevant section of the system specification which is not present in this program?
- Does the description of processing in the program specification tally with that given in the system specification?
- Do the calculations produce sensible results? Are intermediate values explained fully?
- How does the specification cater for links with other programs and processes?
- Does the linkage with other programs tally with the other specifications?
- Are the controls independent of the process they are controlling?
- Does the author of the specification make assumptions about availability and validity of data accessed by this program? What would happen if these assumptions are not realised?
- Has the author considered the possibility of processing, on which this program depends, failing?
- Is there anything missing from the specification which will be needed to complete the program properly, such as file and report layouts?
- Does the program make clear how the program will be run, for example, as part of a suite of programs?
- Is it clear what is needed for the program to be run properly, e.g. operator intervention?
- Is it clear how the program should be tested?

Other processing specifications

The variety of these specifications makes the provision of checklists rather difficult. However, there are a number of obvious checks which can be made, namely those which are suitable for all documents, such as compatibility with source documents.

Checklists suitable for the examples given above are as follows.

JOB STREAMS

- Does the specification provide enough information, including data structures, means of access, program names, etc.?

- Is it possible to write it, given the capabilities of the language which is going to be used?

- Is the processing it performs derived from the system specification with nothing extra or missing or altered?

- Is it clear what should be done if any error is encountered?

- Is it clear how the programs communicate with each other and with the operators?

- Is it clear how successful completion is indicated and what should be done next?

END USER REPORTING

- Are the functions derived from source documents (e.g. the system specification, package documentation) with nothing extra or missing or altered?

- Have all the access rights been clearly set down and approved in writing by the user with authority to do so?

- Is it clear what every category of user can do?

- Is there anything which suggests that rights given to users might lead to breaches of security?

- Will it be clear to users just what data is available to them and what they can do with it?

- Is the data described in terms the users can accept and understand?

- Does the specification provide sufficient information for the person responsible for setting up this function to complete the task?

MENUS

- Are the functions derived from the system specification with nothing extra or missing or altered?

- Does the specification provide sufficient information for the person responsible for setting up this function to complete the task?

- Is what is proposed a basis for a comprehensive, efficient and easy method of using the system and other facilities?
- Does the specification adhere to standards or established practice for menus in the user department and elsewhere?

Program design

- Is the design an accurate reflection of the specification with nothing extra, missing or incorrect?
- Is the design feasible given the programming language which has been selected?
- Will the processing meet any requirements for speed or efficiency?
- Is the program structured in such a way that it will be easy to maintain?
- Will the resulting program access data structures, subprograms and subroutines in the most efficient way, given the processing requirements and the need for clarity?

Program coding

- Is all the coding derived from the program specification and design with nothing else added and no omissions?
- Is any of the coding unclear as to what it is meant to do?
- Are standards observed?
- Is there sufficient documentation? The recommendations of the checklist for writing program code should be considered here.
- Is it apparent which processes depend on others?
- Are the links with other programs clearly defined?
- Is the program coded as efficiently as possible, given the requirement for clarity and ease of maintenance?
- Are there any errors of logic or inefficient use of commands?
- Would a person amending this program be able to find the areas requiring amendment and make the alterations quickly and accurately?

Program test plan

- Is the plan sufficiently comprehensive in view of the criticality of the program? What percentage of possible paths within the program are covered?
- Are all critical and complex processes tested?
- Does the plan cover everything in the recommended list of contents given above?
- Is it apparent what every test is trying to achieve?
- For every test, is it clear what the data should look like before and after the test and how it will change at each stage of the processing?

- Is the plan comprehensive with some tests for every process within the program?

- Are error conditions and internal controls going to be thoroughly tested?

- Is the plan laid out in such a way that each test can be checked off and certified when it has been completed?

- Does it make provision for retesting? This is very important if the program has to be altered during testing. It is possible that the amendment might render earlier tests invalid.

Program test results

- Do the results indicate that the testing has been sufficiently comprehensive?

- Has every planned test actually been carried out?

- Did each test actually prove what it set out to prove?

- Has every test been certified as complete and successful?

- Is supporting documentation adequate? How have tests been dealt with which do not readily provide documentation such as tests on screen handling?

- Was the test data used sufficient for the purpose both in quantity and type? Validation tests should have encompassed minimum and maximum permitted values.

Testing other processing

The same checklists as for program test plans and results can be used here.

System test plan

- Does the plan show who is responsible for each test?

- If more than one testing phase is envisaged, are the aims of each, actions and responsibilities clearly shown?

- Is the scope of the testing comprehensive, including all the facilities which are being provided and every process in the system specification?

- Is the scale of testing adequate in view of the system's role?

- Is the plan laid out so that the completion of each test and the results can be clearly seen?

- Is security included in the testing? For example, what happens if someone tries to process an unauthorised transaction?

- Will the users involved in the testing know what they are doing and when?

- Will the tests prove what they set out to prove?

- Are serious errors needing system recovery procedures included?

- Do the tests reflect the way the system will be used when it has been implemented?

- Is it clear that no test will clash with others and that shared data will be controlled so that the results will not be compromised?

- Is there any feature of the system which is not included in the plan?
- Does the plan take account of the projected availability of programs? Not all will be completed at the same time and some processes may be tested before others.
- What provision is there for repeating tests if necessary?
- Is the data available for testing sufficient for the scale of testing envisaged in the plan?
- All in all, will the tests show if the system will be sufficiently robust to meet the demands placed on it? Include processing peaks, large volumes of data, error recovery, etc.

System test results

- Are the results presented in such a way that readers will be confident of the completeness and validity of the tests? This is especially important if users, who were not involved too deeply in the project, now want to see the results. Excessive technical language should not be needed.
- Do the results show that the test plan has been followed?
- Is there anything to suggest that part of the system may not have been tested properly?
- Has every test been certified?
- Does each test actually prove what it set out to prove?
- Is there sufficient supporting evidence, e.g. reports?
- Is it proven that the system will cope with the amount of processing which will be demanded of it?
- Do the results show any defect or weakness in the system? How can it be rectified?
- Do the results show that the system is a practical means of meeting the requirements of the system proposal?
- Do the results show that the system is ready to be implemented?

End of phase

The phase end, when the results of the system test have been thoroughly analysed and it is agreed by the management of the computer department that the system provides a viable solution.

Users will normally have been involved in the system test and may confirm that the system meets their requirements. However, they should not be expected to express their complete satisfaction at this stage. During the next phase, users have an opportunity to test the system to their own standards. Project staff, including users involved in the project, will judge it against the system specification and system proposal. These users will be familiar with the system but the majority of the user department will not. It will be up to them to decide if the system meets its business requirements during the next phase.

6 Evaluation and acceptance

During the previous two phases, the project team concentrated on building the system with relatively little user involvement. Now both the users and computer operations are brought in again in preparation for the system being implemented. In the first place, the users have to examine the system to make sure that it really does meet their requirements. Then training has to be planned and undertaken so that, from the first day of operation, the new system will become an integral part of their everyday work. Training is also needed for computer operations staff so that they, too, are sufficiently familiar with the system to run it competently.

Unless the implementation of the system is well-planned, problems will inevitably arise. Here, again, cooperation with users and computer operations staff is needed to make sure that everything is handed over at the right time and that everything begins to work when it is supposed to.

Therefore, as soon as this phase begins, the project manager should plan the implementation of the new system and discuss the plan with everyone who has an interest. Obviously the user department should be kept informed but others may need to know what is going on. A new system may affect other people who have had little or nothing to do with its development, since they do not own the system but are merely given access to it.

Take, for example, a system which holds details of exchange rates and which is used by most departments in a company. It may be that they are all familiar with one method of extracting the data for their own purpose. The project manager will have to decide how to inform them of the new system so that they will know when they will start using it. They will also have to know how to use the new system and what to do if they experience any problems. Should the project manager assume that the user department will pass on all necessary information to these users? Maybe it is the responsibility of the user department, but the project manager should at least make certain that steps have actually been taken. Otherwise, the computer department can expect a stream of calls from puzzled users.

Some systems development staff forget that implementing a new system means a lot of work for computer operations. As well as training and familiarisation, scheduling has to be altered, new data structures have to be introduced and old ones altered or deleted. Many systems are replacements for old ones - what should happen to the old data and programs? What special programs have to be run to convert data for the new system? Such questions as these may give the project manager a few headaches even if they are addressed at an early stage during this phase. If postponed or forgotten, the headaches will be a lot worse and shared by many others.

It is as well to tackle implementation planning as soon as possible even if the plan needs alteration later on. Drawing up a good plan and seeing that it is carried out are the keys to successful implementation.

Most would agree that no system is complete unless it has been documented. It is a fact of life, however, that documentation is often given low priority and some systems development staff are only too ready to find an excuse for avoiding it. Suffice to say that a well-documented system will prove more satisfactory to users and operations and project staff will not have to answer questions about the system years after it has been implemented.

Phase initiation

There is no reason why preparatory work on this phase should not begin as soon as the system has been specified in detail. If staff can be spared so that an early start can be made on this phase, so much the better. Therefore, although the activity during this phase has to be completed after Programming and Testing, it may begin while work on that phase is still continuing. However, the experience gained from the system test may well have a bearing on the documentation for users and computer operations so do not expect to complete it until testing is over.

Documents

- Revised project plan
    - Target audience: project team;

       systems manager.

- Implementation plan
    - Target audience: computer operations;

       users;

       project team;

       owners of linked systems;

       computer department management.

- Guidelines for user testing
    - Target audience: users;

       project team.

- User training plan
    - Target audience: users;

       project team;

       training staff;

       external training companies.

- Operations training plan
  - – Target audience: computer operations;

    project team;

    training staff;

    external training companies.
- User system documentation
  - – Target audience: users;

    computer department management;

    systems maintenance staff;

    computer operations.

If there is a 'help' desk, the manager will need copies.

- Operations system documentation
  - – Target audience: computer operations.

No system should be implemented without an implementation plan and system documentation for both users and operations. All should have been formally accepted.

Project plan

This is now revised for the last time.

Revision of the project plan as a whole

- Were the estimates for the Programming and Testing phase accurate? If an early start is made on this phase, i.e. before the Programming and Testing phase was completed, the accuracy of the estimates so far should be considered and re-examined when the previous phase is actually complete.
- Are there implications for the rest of the project, i.e. revised estimates and deadlines?
- Will revision to the timing of the remainder of the project conflict with any externally-imposed time constraints? If so, what can be done either to meet the original deadlines or to revise them?

Detailed planning of the current phase

Consultation will be needed to make sure users and operations staff are available for consultation, training and other activities - all potentially time-consuming.

- What documents are going to be produced during this phase?
- Which staff will work on this phase? What tasks will they perform and when?
- What are the target dates for each activity during this phase, up to and including the implementation of the system?

- Which users will be involved and when?
- What will the roles of the users be?
- Has this had the consent of their managers?
- Which operations staff will be involved and when?
- What will their roles be?
- Has this had the consent of their managers?
- For every activity during this phase:
    - who will be responsible for it;
    - how much time is required for it;
    - when will it start;
    - when will it end;
    - what other tasks depend on it?

During previous phases, much of the project team's work could be seen in terms of the production of documents. During this phase, apart from the system documentation, most documents are plans. Strict adherence to these plans should ensure a successful implementation. The review of the implementation will come during the next phase.

Implementation plan

This important document controls every aspect of system's implementation. It requires the agreement of all involved in the process; the project manager will need both to consult widely in drawing it up and to make sure that it is put into effect. It will help if users and the computer operations manager agree to the plan in writing.

The implementation plan is not merely a schedule of activities: it is a means of communication with all involved in and affected by the new system. Everyone will know what is expected and what others are doing. If the project manager monitors progress closely, for example by regular progress meetings with the team, any possible delays or shortcomings will soon be identified and remedied.

User acceptance testing is a part of this phase and it may be possible to use this activity as a test for some or all of the implementation plan. If a test system representing an old version of a system is converted into a new version, the implementation plan can be tried out and any defects remedied.

Sources

In summary, the project manager should consider the following documents and consult the following people when drawing up the plan.

- Detailed systems specification and related documents and diagrams;
- Project plan;
- Computer operations manager;
- Users especially the user who is the main point of contact in the user department;

- Owners of interfacing systems;
- Project team.

The type of consultation will vary. In particular, the operations manager with other busy schedules will probably tell the project manager how the system will be implemented. Ensuring that this will be acceptable to the users as well may require considerable planning skills not to say diplomacy.

Good communication can determine the success or failure of implementation. The project manager has to consult others and also keep everyone involved abreast of developments. This is not too difficult if everyone is given a copy of the plan with their own role clearly stated. Many companies have electronic mail systems and it is easy to send messages with details of progress or to remind people of what they are supposed to be doing. The project manager should work out who has an interest in the plan, as a source of information, a participant in the implementation process or as someone who needs to know when the system will be available (see Figure 6.1). Having established channels of communication, it is just a question of using them.

Checklist

Not all of the items in the checklist given below will apply to every new system. In all cases dates, people responsible, dependencies and sequences of events must be specified.

General

- Who will be involved in implementation?
- What will their roles be? This will include all those who provide information or who are responsible for some aspect of the implementation.
- When will they be involved?
- Who else needs to know about implementation?
- Have all these interested parties been made aware of their roles and agreed to them?
- How will the project team communicate progress?
- How will the implementation be monitored?

Operational considerations

- When will the implementation take place?
- Has any data to be created for the new system? If so, when, how and by whom will this be done?
- Has any data to be transferred from an earlier version of the system or from other systems? If so, when, how and by whom will this be done?
- Is a phased implementation required? If so, what events will happen at each stage and how will we know if each is successful?

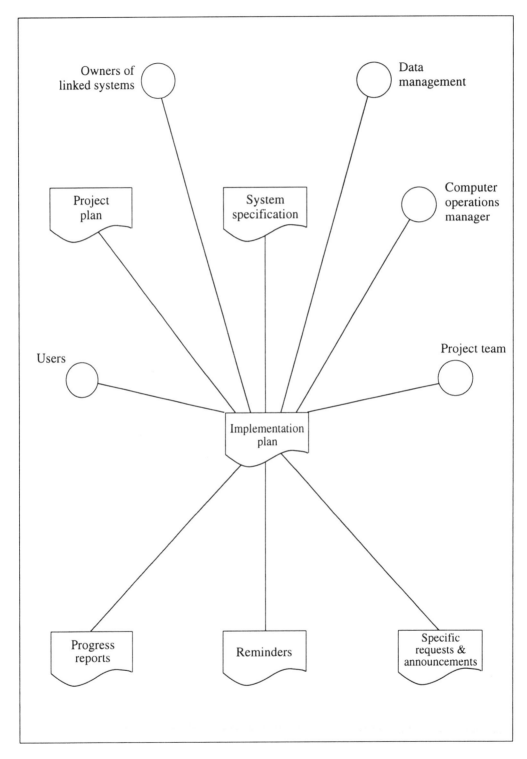

Figure 6.1   Implementation plan

- Is there going to be a period of parallel running? If so,

  - when will this arrangement start and for how long will it be required;

  - how will the parallel systems be controlled;

  - how will the parallel systems interface?

- What arrangements are needed to provide a backup of the old system?

- Is it possible that the old system might need to be reactivated in the event of serious problems? If so, how would it be restored?

- When will it no longer be feasible to return to the old system?

- What new or amended data structures and items will be needed?

- When will these data structures and items be ready?

- Will the old system be held in an archive and, if so, for how long and in what form?

- Which programs, stream jobs and other processing are redundant? What should happen to the sources?

- Which other programs have to be altered or recompiled because of the new system? When will this be complete?

- When will the new programs, jobs and other processing be handed over? When should each be implemented?

- What arrangements will have to be made for the users to access the system?

- Are new logons required? If so, when will they be available? Full details of access rights and authorisation should be present.

- Will there be any special arrangements for monitoring the system? If so, how will this be done, who will set them up and when will the arrangements cease?

- If other systems are affected in any way, have steps been taken to make sure that they are changed in parallel with the implementation of the new system?

- Have all users who will be affected in any way by the new system been advised of the new system, its implications for them and the date of implementation?

- What are the arrangements for pre-implementation training? When is it due to begin and end? Who will be trained and who will provide the training?

- When will operational documentation be handed over?

- When will computer operations have completed all their preparatory work, including training, scheduling, handovers, setting up archive files etc?

- What are the channels of communication between the project team and computer operations?

- When will new hardware and software have to be installed?

Users

- Has authorisation been given for all logons and access rights to the new system?
- Is a period of user acceptance testing planned? If so:
  - when is it due to begin and end;
  - who is responsible for stating whether or not it is successful;
  - what facilities are needed for the testing and how will they be provided?
- Who is responsible for formally accepting the system and when is the decision due?
- Are any users responsible for creating new data, parameters, etc. for the new system to start functioning? If so, who are they, how will the work be done and when is it due to be completed?
- What are the arrangements for pre-implementation training? When is it due to begin and end? Who will be trained?
- When will the users have completed all their preparatory work, including training, creating data and security administration?
- When will the user documentation be handed over?
- What are the channels of communication between the project team and users?
- How will the user department cope with using a new system at the same time as coping with all its other work?

Legal/contractual

- Have all contracts for new software, hardware etc. been signed and, if not, when will this he done?
- If registration under data protection legislation is needed or any other legal measures have to be taken, when will this be completed?

Guidelines for user testing

How will the users know that the system measures up to the requirements? If they do not assess this prior to implementation, the project team may be faced with requests for instant changes during the first critical days of the new system's life. A presentation of the system test results and demonstrations will help only insofar as it proves the system works. Most systems are interactive and need to be used in a simulated business context so that users can satisfy themselves that they perform their intended function. If this approach is taken two things are required: the first is a suitable test environment which mirrors the future system accurately, albeit on a smaller scale; the second is guidance so the testing is conducted methodically.

Although the work involved in setting up a test environment may be considerable, it can also serve a second, very useful purpose. The implementation plan can be tried out and revised if necessary. Alternatively, the systems test environment may be good enough to double up for user acceptance testing. The test environment will also be useful for training purposes, indeed the familiarity with the system which the users will gain from user acceptance testing may be regarded as part of training. However, the aims of user acceptance testing and user training are distinct and one should not be considered as a substitute for the other.

How much of the system should be tested in this way? This will depend on the users who must make themselves available and be committed to testing the system thoroughly. Only the user responsible for the acceptance of the system can decide the precise scope of the testing. If the system contains many features of an older version, it may be necessary only to test the new processes. Also, the user may decide to leave out parts of the system which are rarely used, for example annual processing. At the very least, the user should be convinced that day-to-day working with the new system, including documentation, will actually achieve the system's objectives laid down in the statement of requirements.

The project manager should not simply provide a testing environment and let the user get on with testing unaided, especially if the user has little or no previous experience. By drawing up guidelines for the users – with their participation and agreement – the project manager can help the users. A further requirement for success is that the project manager should be able to see the system from the users' point of view so that the user acceptance testing will also be conducted from that viewpoint. There is no virtue in having user acceptance testing which reproduces system or program testing.

The project manager can also assist in analysing results and indicating the limitations of this kind of testing. For example, the user test environment will probably use a smaller amount of data than the final system and will also have fewer people using it at the same time. The response time may be better in the test environment than in the live environment. If a certain level of performance was specified in the requirements, it may be easily met in the test environment. The project manager should make it clear that false conclusions can be made and provide more realistic estimates of live performance.

The checklist given here, all from the user's point of view, should be used to prepare a list of tests. It must be made clear that the users will actually test and the project team will provide support only. Attempts to perform user acceptance testing for the users because they are too busy is a waste of time.

- What am I testing here? It must be seen as part of my department' s activities, i.e. a business process and not simply as a computer process.

- What needs to be done to prove that the system will really enable me to perform a business activity? A number of computer processes may be needed, such as accessing screens, inputting data, printing reports and so on. having broken each business function down into a number of computer processes, what are these computer processes and what do I have to do to make them work properly? This may involve some or all of:

  - inputting, amending and deleting data;
  - updating master files;
  - inputting parameters;
  - choosing options on a screen menu or by function keys;
  - checking reports;
  - checking controls.

- Where does the process demand communication with other people and other systems? How can this be tested? Examples are:
  - communicating with computer operations so that they run a program;
  - communication between staff and supervisors where the latter must authorise a transaction or update a master file;
  - communicating with another system so that I can read one of its files;
  - asking someone at another site to pass on a file via a network.
- Does each function being tested really do what I want it to do?
- What happens if I press the wrong key, if I forget to do something or commit some other human error? Does the system make clear:
  - that an error has occurred;
  - what the error is in terms that I can understand;
  - what I have to do to correct the error;
  - what the effect the error might have on the system and other users?
- Does the system make me correct such errors? If not, what are the reasons?
- Are the instructions in the draft user documentation and the 'help' facilities really helpful? Are they clear, comprehensive, comprehensible and free from computer jargon?

  (The acid test is this - do I need to go to the computer department for an explanation every time I look at a manual or 'help' screen?)
- Is the system convenient to use? In particular:
  - is it easy to go from one screen to another and back again, especially frequently used screens;
  - when I use the system for a business activity, is this convenient in view of the sequence of operations on each screen and the sequence of the screens;
  - is it quite clear what the contents of every field on each screen contains;
  - are running totals and other calculations screen correct and do they serve a useful purpose;
  - are reports clear, correct and useful;
  - is it easy to interrupt and abandon an operation if I want to do so?
- Does each user of the system only get the facilities to which he or she is entitled?
- Are there any apparent security weaknesses? For example, might it be-possible to bypass controls, tamper with data or read reports without authority?
- Do the audit functions work properly, giving no more or less access than they are supposed to?
- What cannot be achieved by my own testing? What do I need to do in order to find out how to ensure that requirements are met?

User training plan

The aim of this training plan is to ensure that the user department will be able to work normally with the aid of their new computer system and derive the full benefits they were meant to achieve from it. Training should include practical sessions and the opportunity for users to become familiar with all the processes they will use in their work. Training should always be slanted towards teaching the individual how to use the system in his or her job – or groups of individuals performing the same sort of role rather than providing a general purpose survey of all the facilities of the system. Such a survey will only be of use by way of introduction.

As well as guided training sessions, consideration should be given to providing a test system where the users can practice as they learn.

The training should address only what is needed. If the new system is much the same as an old version or is a subsystem added to an existing one, there will be a lot of familiar ground. There is no point in teaching people what they know already and, in these circumstances, a few sessions demonstrating the new facilities will probably suffice. At the other extreme, users who have never used a computer system before will need a lot of help in finding their way round menus and in learning how to write records on a screen, even in basic keyboard skills.

The following checklist should be considered.

- Who are the users and when will they be available for training?

- Has the cost of the training been agreed with the user department ?

- Can we group them to make training easier (e.g. by function)?

- Where some facilities are performed by a group of users, who also have different tasks as well, can the training sessions be combined?

- Which users have experience of computer systems?

- To what extent are the users familiar with the type of equipment they need in order to use the new system? Is there any type of hardware or software which is new to them? If, for example, personal computers are being used for the first time, additional training in PC familiarisation, security procedures, etc. will be needed.

- If the system is a replacement, in what ways does it differ from the old one?

- Will the users perform the same tasks as before using a new system or is their type of work going to change as well?

- Which functions need the cooperation of users and communciation between them?

- Which functions require communication outside of the user department, e.g. with computer operations?

- Which functions are difficult and may therefore need special attention?

- Which functions are especially easy and may perhaps be omitted, unless they are very important?

- Which functions involve familiarity with equipment, office products, etc? Some users may not be used to printers especially if pre-printed stationery is involved.

- Which functions are only used occasionally and perhaps will not be required for months, e.g. year-end processing? Is training needed now?
- Is the user documentation available, at least in a draft form, and can it be used in the training?
- Is any supplementary training needed, e.g. in security? Staff not familiar with on-line systems should be aware of the importance of keeping passwords secret, not using other people's access rights and so on.
- When will computer department staff be ready either to train or to assist in the training?
- Who will perform the training? Training in the use of a package may involve the supplier.
- If external training is needed, when can it be arranged?
- If the system accesses remote systems, receives data from or transmits data to other companies, databases or installations, is training for the users at the other site needed? Consideration should be given to this especially if the remote sites play an important role in making the system effective.

Operations training plan

Computer operations staff play a vital role in computer systems. They need to be trained so that they fully understand the day-to-day running of the system, can deal correctly with any emergencies and appreciate why they have to perform certain functions. The training should not be regarded as a substitute for well-written, thorough system documentation. However, it should assist operations staff in drawing up their own schedules. Most computer operations departments have standard procedures for their work: training should acknowledge this and concentrate on any special requirements or actions which they must take.

- When will operations staff be available for training?
- Who will provide the training? Is an external training needed?
- What programs or suites of programs have to be run regularly?
- If there are any background jobs, what is their function and when should they be run?
- When do backup copies of data have to be taken, in addition to those taken regularly as part of the installation's standard security procedures?
- Who are the users with whom regular contact is most likely?
- How will users request reports, programs or other activities needing operator intervention?
- Which programs can be run on request?
- When will operators have to create or modify parameters?
- What other actions will operators have to perform when running programs or suites of programs?
- When is special stationery required? Who is responsible for maintaining supplies of it?

- Does pre-printed stationery present any special problems?

- What are the volumes of data and run times for regular suites of programs such as month-end procedures?

- Is any of the hardware or software unfamiliar? If so, when can training be arranged?

  Is there a 'help desk'? If so, what training do its staff need so that they will be able to assist the users of the new system?

- Does the system interface with others at remote sites? If so consideration should be given to training these staff if their role is not going to be easily understood. The following are particularly important:

  - systems availability;

  - data to be provided by or for the new system;

  - format of data;

  - system controls;

  - communications and contacts, especially for emergencies and problems.

User system documentation

Accessibility and problem orientation are the two considerations which should be paramount when designing documentation for users. They should be able to find out what they need to know as quickly as possible. When they have found the specific information they need, it should be directed towards solving their problems. This may sound obvious but unfortunately much system documentation is virtually worthless, mainly because it is too often seen as an irksome task to be done as an afterthought.

Previously, the 'bible' approach was preferred. This meant that a luckless, junior member of the project team was charged with producing a thick tome describing every process in great detail. Such manuals rarely helped a user who wanted to know what he or she actually had to do in order to make the system work - even if it did it was probably incomprehensible except to other computer specialists. Never updated, they ended up gathering dust on a shelf or consigned to the manager's desk drawer.

User documentation is not likely to consist of a single document. For any on-line system an on-line 'help' facility should always be considered. Another approach is to produce cards or small handbooks which can be left on desks or placed in a pocket on the side of a terminal. Some users will have extra facilities and responsibilities such as supervision of the system or running special programs. It is better to deal with them by writing specific documentation. The average user should not need to plough through all the year-end and month-end facilities in order to discover what an error code is on his or her input screen.

The on-line 'help' facility will have been designed as part of the system. Some of its contents may have been added during programming or left until now. Some may be included as part of a package but even this may need to be supplemented. The following checklist should be considered.

- Is this process on-line and shared by many users? If so, it should be included as part of the on-line 'help' facility.

- What will a user need to know in order to be able to access and manipulate data? Consider:
  - how to explain the significance of each field;
  - how to go from field to field on a screen;
  - how to go from one screen to another;
  - how to tell the user what constitutes valid input;
  - how to explain how fields can be edited;
  - how to tell the user that an error has occurred elsewhere in the system;
  - how to explain what function keys do.
- Does a screen run other programs? As well as the list above, consider:
  - what the parameters are;
  - what the effect of the program is;
  - what else the user must do (e.g. telling others in the user department, checking output).
- Does the process invoked by this screen involve using other equipment, special stationery, etc? If so, consider providing information on how to use it. For example, if the program will print to preprinted stationery on a printer attached to the terminal, the user might not always be too clear about lining-up the stationery correctly.

Consider the following checklist for printed documentation.

- What business function does each process perform?
- Which processes or programs have to be taken together to complete a process?
- Which processes does the user need to invoke in order to do something, for example, run a report?
- Which functions require contact with computer operations? State:
  - who should be contacted;
  - what should be asked for (e.g. the title of a suite of programs);
  - when it can be requested;
  - what the user must do (e.g. written authorisation).
- What checks have to be carried out when a process is complete?
- Does the system have an audit facility? If so, its use should be explained.

Operations system documentation

Although it is useful for operations staff to have some idea about the purpose of a system, they are mainly concerned with making the system work efficiently and effectively for the users and without impinging on other systems which share the same hardware.

The only operations staff who will need to know the same sort of information as the users are those who provide a 'help' desk service and they should be able to get most of their information from the user system documentation.

Operations manager are responsible for planning. They need to be able to draw up schedules, especially at times when the demand on computing resources is heavy. The new system is generally one among many and its processing has to be slotted in among the others.

Statistical information about run times, volumes of data are very useful. A clear description of the system in terms of suites of programs, input and output and operator actions will go a long way to providing a sound basis.

At the other extreme is the computer room. Here swift action is needed, especially if something goes wrong. Operators need to be provided with enough information to know precisely what has to be done when any program is run and what to do if things go wrong. Error messages generated by the program may say what has gone wrong - but what should the operator do about it?

The answer may not be obvious especially when the message is a standard one provided by the manufacturer's software. Let us say that the operator is running a suite of programs and is confronted with a message which says that a database has been filled to capacity and that, consequently, the program is going to terminate. What should the operator do? Should the whole suite of programs be abandoned? If so, does the database have to be restored to its original state before the program began - or even earlier? Should the operator increase the database's capacity and start again? If so, by how much and in what circumstances? If the database has suddenly doubled in size there may well be some underlying fault, perhaps a program error. Increasing the capacity might compound the error.

These and other decisions are sometimes faced by relatively inexperienced operators. It is not enough to say that the operator should ask someone. At 4 a.m. there will probably be nobody to ask. Having to ring around the home phone numbers of people who might know the answer is not a satisfactory way of running computer operations.

The advice, therefore, and this originated from somebody with years of experience, is to imagine that an inexperienced operator with no knowledge of the system has to run your programs in the middle of the night completely unaided. Will he or she be able to read your documentation and know what to do, even if things go wrong? A brief, clear description, preferably on a single sheet, with actions prescribed for all possible events will be much appreciated.

Therefore, operations system documentation has two aims: planning for which a manual is suitable and running programs and suites of programs for which brief, lucid documents are needed.

The following checklist should be used when compiling the operations manual.

- What hardware, operating systems and networks are used by the system?

- What software packages, including applications packages are used by the system?

- For each of the above, what sources of information are available e.g. manuals, suppliers' 'help' desks?

- For each of the above, who should be contacted in the event of an emergency and how?

- What are the physical storage requirements of the system? As well as disc space, consider other media such as magnetic tape.

- What is the anticipated growth of these requirements?
- Will there be any times when extra storage capacity might be required? If so, when is this likely to occur and what sort of capacity might be needed?
- What data will be sent to archives and when?
- How long will data remain in the archives?
- Where will it be held?
- What media will be used for the archives?
- When is archive data likely to be needed?
- How quickly will data have to be brought back from the archives?
- When do backup copies of the system's data have to be taken - in addition to those required by installation standards?
- What are the logging requirements?
- What background or housekeeping programs have to be run and when?
- When will the system be on-line i.e. between which hours each day?
- Are there any special requirements for fast access?
- When are peaks and troughs of on-line usage anticipated?
- What are the initial capacities of the data structures?
- What are their anticipated normal growth rates?
- When are these growth rates likely to be exceeded and by how much?
- For each of the programs suites of programs in the system:
  - what does each do;
  - when are they run;
  - what determines that they are run;
  - what parameters are needed and who provides them;
  - how long do they take;
  - how do they affect the system's data structures (including capacities);
  - what are the media requirements;
  - what special stationery is needed;
  - what output is produced (include volumes);
  - what happens to the output;
  - what should be done in the event of an internal error;
  - what should be done in the event of an external problem causing the system to fail, e.g. network failure;
  - what recovery procedures must be followed?

- What *ad hoc* programs are there?

- What special security arrangements are needed?

- Who is responsible for granting access rights?

- Who is allowed to run programs?

Some of the security arrangements should be covered by the company's security procedures, for example, how authorisation to run programs is passed from user to operations manager. It is shown here for completion.

The following should be considered when writing the instructions for operators. They apply to both individual programs and suites of programs, both batch and on-line.

- What determines that this process can begin?

- What media are needed?

- What ancillary equipment is needed e.g. printers and stationery?

- If the stationery is pre-printed, how is it lined up?

- What does the operator have to do when before it can begin (e.g. put up a scratch tape, take a backup)?

- On which processes does this one depend and how will the operator know if they have worked properly?

- What parameters are needed and where do they come from?

- What has to be done with the output? Include the destination of printed output and the means of sending it there.

- Which data structures does the process access? Note those which are modified in any way.

- How long does the process take?

- How does the operator know whether it was completely successful?

- What informs the operator that an error has occurred?

- What should the operator do in the event of an error? Include what should be done with output which has already been generated. Confidential reports may have to be shredded.

- What processes depend on this one?

- How will the operator know whether to continue with the next processes?

- What should the operator do in the event of an external failure, i.e. one not caused by the internal workings of the system such as a power failure? There should be a standard recovery procedure but exceptional procedures may be required in some special cases.

Obviously there is some duplication between the operators' instructions and the operations manual. However, it will be noted that the majority of the former are guidance for action.

Review

Implementation plan

- Is it clear from the plan that there is:
  - somebody responsible for every action;
  - a time by which the action must be completed;
  - a means of communicating with others regarding progress and completion of the action;
  - a means of ascertaining whether or not the action was completed successfully?
- Has the plan been approved by all interested parties, especially computer operations and the users?
- Does each task appear feasible in the time allocated for it and with the staff allocated to it?
- Where actions depend on others, is it clear what will happen if something is not completed on time? For example, if training is not completed when it is supposed to be, what effect would that have on the implementation?
- Is there anything to suggest that normal working might be interrupted by the implementation? Consider this not only for the users and computer operations but for others who depend on them for a service.
- Are there any omissions, duplications or inconsistencies in the plan? For example, do activities involving the same individuals overlap? Are new programs going to be handed over to coincide with the introduction of new or amended data structures?
- Does the plan provide for the transfer of data from an old system to the new one and other steps to ensure that data will be ready when the system begins operation?
- How does the plan provide for checking that data will be complete and consistent when the system is implemented?
- How does the plan provide for checking that all programs and processes will be present when the system is implemented?
- Does the system provide for a resumption of the old system if implementation fails? If so, is it a realistic possibility? Does it show in detail what steps will have to be taken?
- What will happen to old backup copies of the old system? How will they be accessed should the need arise?
- Does the plan also provide for a final copy of the old system to be taken? If so:
  - where will it be held;
  - how long will it be kept;
  - how will it be accessed?
- Does the system include a regular cycle of processing? If so:
  - does the plan include a timetable for at least the first period;

- was this drawn up by or approved by computer operations;
- does it have the user department's agreement?

• Is there going to be a period of parallel running? If so:

- when is it due to end;
- who or what will determine that it should end;
- is there a plan for disposing of the old system?

• Are any testing environments accessed by the users (e.g. for training or acceptance) going to be maintained? If so, when will they be deleted?

• Is the implementation plan consistent with the project plan? Given the timescales for implementation, is it realistic?

Guidelines for user testing

It is sometimes difficult for computer professionals to see things from a user perspective. Rather than provide guidance for the users on how to test the system to see if it does what it is meant to do in business terms, the project team may be tempted to provide a re-hash of the system test plan. This is not to say that techniques for testing should not be included and any aids to clarity such as worked examples will be beneficial. It is really a question of focus.

• Are the guidelines written from a user perspective?

• Do they test business processes or computer processes?

• Are all the processes part of the system, traceable to source documents?

• Do they provide a means for the users to test the new system unaided?

• If the users follow the guidelines, will they be able to judge whether or not the system meets their requirements?

• Are the guidelines written with the particular needs of this user department in mind, concentrating on their problems, working methods etc?

• If some of the users are not regular users of computer systems, do the guidelines provide enough information and assistance?

• Are the guidelines written without computer jargon?

• Have users seen the guidelines and confirmed that they are understandable and sufficient?

• Are the guidelines complete? When compared with the statement of requirements and systems proposal, does it appear that any part of the system has been omitted from the user testing? If so, there may be a good reason but it should be made clear.

• Do the guidelines attempt to tell users what to test rather than give advice on how to test?

• Do the guidelines attempt to make up the users' mind on such matters as what test data is needed, the relative importance of each test and the way the results should be interpreted?

- Is there anything to suggest that the guidelines are steering the user's attention to some parts of the system only? Is there any reason for this? Care should be taken to make sure that a user has a chance to test even parts of the system which might prove less satisfactory than others. For example, although the requirements may not have laid down anything about screen handling for part of the system, the project team may be well aware that it is not very easy to use.

- Is the use of documentation, on-line 'help' facility, error processing recommended as part of the testing? The users may have overlooked these if not included in their requirements.

User training plan

Here the two key issues are comprehensiveness and user orientation. The aim is to make sure that sufficient numbers of staff in the user department are trained for the system to be used properly and effectively from the day of implementation. This should include supervisory staff and others who have to perform special functions unavailable to others. It is a breach of security if the office junior has to be brought in to manage the system controls because his boss "did not have time" for training.

- Does the plan include a timetable giving the following information:
  - who is being trained;
  - the aim and subject of the training;
  - when and where the training is going to take place;
  - who is giving the training?
- Are there any clashes with any other plans?
- Is it clear where external resources are providing training? This should include both 'on-site' and 'off-site' training.
- Is the training plan comprehensive, addressing:
  - all processes which make up the system;
  - the interfaces and relationships between processes;
  - the relationship of different types of data to each other (e.g. master and transaction files, dependencies, etc.);
  - system security;
  - error handling;
  - action to be taken when problems arise;
  - the documentation;
  - channels of communication?
- Is the emphasis of the training programme towards the user department's business activity, showing how tasks will be performed with the help of the new system?

- Does the plan take into account the use each individual will make of the system?
- Will a sufficient number of staff be trained so that. the system can be used effectively from the date of implementation? If there is any doubt about this, the user should be informed.
- Is the training representative in that instruction will be provided in all of the system's functions?
- Does the plan take into account the varying levels of experience and computer expertise of those using the system?
- Does the plan take into account new software or new equipment which is being introduced with the new system?
- Is it possible that training will not be as complete as it should be? For example, are a sufficient number of managers and supervisors going to be trained?
- Is training in all security operations and controls included? This should be present both for those with security functions as part of their job and for those unfamiliar with the security practices needed for new equipment.
- Is it clear how much it will cost and who is paying for it? External training can be expensive and the users should know how much they will have to spend.

Operations training plan

For some systems, using familiar hardware and software and performing familiar processing, most operations staff will need no more than a general survey of the new system and its main processes. It helps to concentrate on new technology and ways of doing things which have not been seen before. The reason why things are being done the way they are should also be given.

- Does the plan include a timetable giving the following information:
  - who is being trained;
  - the aim and subject of the training;
  - when and where the training is going to take place;
  - who is giving the training?
- Are there any clashes with any other plans?
- Is it clear where external resources are providing training? This should include both 'on-site' and 'off-site' training.
- Does the plan deal with all major areas of operations? In particular:
  - does it explain when and why there might be processing peaks;
  - does it describe all the suites of programs, especially those which are run regularly and frequently;
  - does it focus on processes where a high degree of operator involvement is needed;
  - does it always show exactly how operations will be involved in any process;
  - does it include guidance with the documentation?

- Does the plan concentrate on features of this type of system which will be unfamiliar to the operations staff?
- Does it explain why things are done the way they are?
- Are the channels of communication with the users and with other systems explained?
- Will sufficient operations staff be trained in order to run the system efficiently from the date of implementation.
- Will the future planning of operations procedures be made easier by this training?

User system documentation

Reviewing the user system documentation can be quite difficult because the documentation may be spread over different documents and some may be held as an on-line 'help' facility. If possible, though, it should all be reviewed together in order to assess its completeness more easily.

The first questions in the checklist given below deal with the sort of use you would expect to make of an on-line 'help' facility. Putting yourself in the place of a user who is not a habitual user of computers, would you be able to do your job properly with the aid of the on-line 'help' facility? Reviewing with a member of the user department will be beneficial.

- Is everything expressed clearly without recourse to computer jargon?
- Do the messages show how business processes should be performed?
- If one process depends on another, does it tell the user what has to be done in order to invoke the second process? For example, if a transaction file has to be validated against a master file, a basic error message saying something of the nature of "mismatch error on PROFMAST" is not particularly helpful. If the user then invokes the 'help' facility and is told "record not present on master file", this may help a little more but not a lot. It would be better if the error message said something like;

"There is no matching record for this code on the profit centre master file. Try <HELP>."

The 'help' message might say;

"All valid profit centre codes must be present on the profit centre master file. If the code you used was an error, please try again with the correct code. If you need to create a new profit centre, press function key 2. This will enable you to update the master file and return to the update screen."

The above assumes that the user is authorised to create master file records, otherwise the message would perhaps state that the master file controller should be contacted.

- Is every process covered by the 'help' facility?
- Have the needs of different type, of user:, been taken into account?

Next, consider the printed documentation.

- Is it clear how all the business processes are handled by the system?

- If a user has to communicate with computer operations, for example to get a program run, is the terminology used here compatible with that used in the operational documentation?

- Are all dependencies shown?

- Is the effect of each process made clear? Could there be any doubt as to the permanent nature of some updating processes? It is particularly important that senior users, who can decide when major updates are run, fully appreciate the consequences of their actions. Systems may have controls built into them to prevent some disastrous errors, for example running a year end close program before the final month has been processed. Systems can also sometimes be restored from backups. But recovery is sometimes very difficult or impossible and it is surely better if the user understands the full implications of a process.

- Are the systems controls fully explained and the risks of not observing them made clear?

- Will the users be able to make full use of the system without frequently asking the computer department for help because they do not understand what is going on?

- Is everything described relevant and traceable to the source documents?

Operations system documentation

The goal is for computer operations staff to be able to do their work properly without having to chase systems development staff to find out what they should be doing. The ability to make decisions and to act promptly is a necessary part of operations work: the documentation should assist in this.

The operations manual has to be comprehensive but also laid out in such a way that a reader can find any information without too much trouble. If it is held on-line, keyword searching may make this easier. Otherwise a good index or at least a very detailed table of contents should be looked for. The systems specification should be used as a source document when reviewing the manual. The following checklist should also be consulted. If a representative of computer operations can be brought into the review, so much the better.

- Is the operations manual comprehensive and sufficiently detailed? Looking back at the checklist for preparing the manual, has anything been omitted without good reason?

- When compared with the systems specification, does the manual cover every process?

- Does the manual show what the role of operations is for each process? Does it contain any extraneous material?

- Assuming you had to plan a schedule for computer operations, would the manual provide you with enough information to be able to do so? Remember that you will have to do at least some of the following tasks:

  - decide when programs and suites of programs can be run;

  - arrange for backups to be taken;

  - order stationery, magnetic tapes, etc;

- monitor capacities;
- receive input and dispatch output;
- keep in touch with users and the staff at other installations;
- take into account the need, of other systems and users;
- act fast and make changes if problems occur or if priorities change.

• Is the description of regular processing clear and comprehensive? Will it be possible to do everything in the timescales prescribed?

• Are all channels of communication explained?

• If a user speaks about something in the user system documentation will the reference be apparent to the reader of the operations system documentation? Imagine the potential confusion if the user says "I want you to run the first part of the budget centre monthly analysis' and the operations system documentation does not use this descriptions. Whoever is scheduling might look at the budget centre monthly analysis, find the first suite of programs and run it, not knowing that the first part comprises three suites of programs.

• From a security point of view, is there any risk of highly confidential data being treated like any other data? Consider, for example, the distribution of reports.

• Are the arrangements for security backup and recovery sufficient?

When considering the operator instructions, the method recommended when compiling them should be used again. It will also be helpful if an operator is brought into the review to consider some realistic scenarios.

• Assume you have to make decisions about the program or suite of programs being run here. Is it quite clear what you should do if any error occurs? Let us say that the second of a suite of three programs has failed. Would you:

- just make a note in the log and carry on;
- abandon or run the rest of the programs in this suite;
- abandon or run programs or suites of programs which follow this one;
- try to correct the error;
- know how and where to report the error;
- try to restart the program;
- take a copy of the data structures after the error;
- know what to do with any output produced by the program in error or previous programs in the suite;
- restore the data structures to the state they were in before the program in error, before the suite began or before the previous suite of programs began?

• Assume you have to make decisions about the program or suite of programs being run here but this time all goes well. Do you:

- understand what has to be done next;

- know what had to be done before the suite could begin and know how to ascertain how the previous process was successful;

- know what tapes stationery, etc., were required;

- know what to do with the output;

- know who to tell about the result of the process;

- know what has to be done next?

- Is there anything inconsistent with security requirements? For example, are confidential reports treated differently from others?

- Are all processes represented here and are they all mentioned in the operations manual?

- Does the processing match that laid down in the system specification?

End of phase

This phase will be complete when everything in the implementation plan has been done. In short,

- having evaluated the system against their requirements, the users accept the system and make such changes to their working methods as are necessary in preparation for the implementation;

- all those who are affected in any way by the new system are advised of the implementation;

- computer operations have revised their work schedules and are fully conversant with the operational requirements of the system;

- all new and amended data structures have been set up and data has been altered or input as necessary;

- new hardware and software is ready;

- everyone who needs to be trained has been trained;

- all the documentation has been handed over and accepted;

- the system has been successfully handed over and live running has begun.

Only the meanest of project managers would begrudge a further item at this stage, namely a modest celebration.

A consideration of the success of the implementation, and therefore of its planning and all the activities which made up this phase, will be dealt with next, preferably after the system has been running for an agreed period.

Systems are sometimes handed over in haste and important activities (especially documentation) are postponed. It is difficult to avoid these situations always. But it is wrong to say that a system has been implemented just because the computer part of it is working, even though it is the most important part. This phase - and the system - should not be considered complete until all activities have been finished.

7 Post-implementation

The project. is complete and the system is, we hope, providing a good service. Now is the chance for some retrospection. Is the system as good as it should be? Does the experience of the project have any lessons for us? During this phase two distinct but related topics are considered. The first is to take a hard look at the newly implemented system and decide if it does what it was supposed to do. The second is to look back over the project and consider whether the process ensured that a sufficiently high level of quality was built into the system.

Most new computer systems are reviewed after they have been running for a time, frequently because they are not satisfactory. A more positive approach is to monitor the new system not only to investigate whether the system is working properly but also to see what benefits it has brought .

A post-implementation review should have been planned during the Definition phase. Users will then have the satisfaction of knowing that the computer department will continue to take an active interest in their new system. It also means that project staff, who will be working on a new system when the post-implementation review is held, will know that they will be required for consultation. Another benefit is that the prospect of a post-implementation review can be used to justify a moratorium on amendments to the system until it has been completed – although errors will, of course, have to be corrected.

Computer staff are sometimes reluctant to reconsider a project, especially if the review is a few months after the system was implemented. It is important, therefore, that a retrospective examination of the project should not be perceived as an exercise in fault-finding. Moreover, we are not only looking at what could be done better but at what was done well and which should be emulated in other projects. The way the project was managed, the relative success of the techniques used may all be considered here.

The systems manager may decide to carry out these reviews alone or ask an independent quality assurance expert to conduct the review. There is no reason why they should not be entrusted to the project manager or one of the project team so long as the results are seen to be objective. When the documents are reviewed, care should be taken to make sure that any attempts at finding scapegoats, indulging in self-praise or playing company politics are excluded. Needless to say, the views of all those who took part in the project should be considered.

But what if something turns up which suggests that the project has been hindered by an individual, for example, if it is apparent that someone has not worked properly? In fact, it is most unlikely that anything serious will not have been noticed long before. If the project manager found that a member of staff was bone idle, he or she will have taken steps to put matters right. The reports may refer to problems of ability or whatever but should not name individuals. Rather they should state what needs to be done to reduce the risk of the same thing happening again.

Phase initiation

The post-implementation review can begin as soon as the system becomes fully operational. However, useful data is only likely to become available after the users have become familiar with the system and, if nothing else, used to it. The easiest way to control this properly is to agree a date for the review to begin and end before the system is actually implemented. The review commencement date will begin the phase.

Documents

Two documents should be written during this phase, although their content may give rise to others, for example, a recommendation that departmental standards should be changed or that the user department should be approached with a view to improving channels of communication. They may be some of the most influential documents produced during the life cycle since they may affect departmental policy in important considerations such as future choice of software and hardware.

The post-implementation system review considers how well the statement of requirements and quality objectives have been met. It also addresses problems which have arisen since implementation, seeking out the causes and recommending improvements. Any changes to the system will become part of the agreed change management procedures. Although the report must be frank, it should not blame individuals for problems but look for ways of making improvements.

The post-implementation project review looks back at how well the project was run. Here, too, problem areas should be investigated and possible improvements considered. It should be written in conjunction with the post-implementation system review since the latter will contain data useful in evaluating the project.

Post-implementation system review

- Target audience: users;

  computer department management;

  all those working on the project.

Post-implementation project review

- Target audience: computer department management;

  all those working on the project.

Post-implementation system review

The source documents for this document are as follows.

- A record of all errors or urgent problems which have occurred since implementation. A computer department normally maintains this information as a matter of course as part of its service to its users, e.g. as a 'help desk'.

- A 'wish list' of all improvements which the users and other interested parties such as computer operations consider necessary or desirable.

- The systems documentation.

People who should be consulted are representatives of the user department (including those performing different roles, using different parts of the system) and computer staff. The latter should include operations and staff maintaining the system in any way, for example, correcting errors or explaining how it works.

All those consulted should be asked to provide as much useful information as possible. It is not enough to discover that the system is slow sometimes. You need to know rather more detail if the report is going to make a soundly-based recommendation for improving matters, or even simply to explain. When is it slow? How long is it slow for? What are the consequences of these response problems? Why is it slow? Such a complaint from a user might result in changes to the system to improve response or a recommendation that the user department should change its working practices.

The following checklist should be considered when conducting the review and writing the report.

- Does the system satisfy the needs laid down in the statement of requirements? If not, what are the shortcomings?

- How has the system performed when compared with the systems proposal? If there are any problems, what are they and where and when do they occur?

- Was the system changed after implementation? If so:
  - how many errors had to be corrected;
  - how many changes were made because the system was unsatisfactory in some way;
  - how were users and computer operations affected?

- Was it necessary to return to an earlier system at any stage? Was this during or after the implementation period?

- Do the number of requests for changes to the system suggest that the system does not measure up to the statement of requirements or system proposal?

- Were the benefits given as justification for the system realised? Include all benefits including intangible ones if sufficient time has elapsed for them to become apparent.

- Apart from meeting any specific criteria laid down in the statement of requirements and other documents, is the system easy to use? Does it provide useful, accurate data when needed?

- After training, did users and operations staff feel confident about using the system? Did subsequent experience justify their opinions?

- Have the documentation and 'help' facilities enabled the users and operations staff to find answers to most of their queries?
- What do the users think of the documentation, 'help' facility etc?
- What do computer operations staff think of their documentation? Has it enabled them to work unaided without having to ask project staff?
- When did former members of the project team have to get involved in the live system and why?
- Has every part of the system been used? If not, why not?
- If there are complaints about the system, to what facilities or processes do they refer? Include interfaces with other systems, 'end-user' reporting and other *ad hoc* facilities.
- In spite of any shortcomings, are the users confident that they can work with the new system?
- Does the user department use the facilities provided in the way they were intended? In particular, are systems controls being used properly?
- Have there been any reported breaches of security, including attempted breaches? If so:
  - were they accidental or deliberate;
  - was any serious damage caused;
  - how did they happen;
  - if countermeasures existed, to what extent did they work?
- Are the users and computer operations staff confident that the system controls and security features actually provide the level of security the system is meant to have?
- What parts of the system function really well? Why are they judged to be especially good?
- Has the system brought any benefits which were not anticipated?

While the report should not gloss over any shortcomings, success should also be noted.

Post-implementation project review

The source documents for this review are the same as for the post-implementation system review. If the latter has been written by a different author, it should itself be consulted as it will provide insight into the reaction of all interested parties and will mean that the same questions do not have to be asked twice.

The post-implementation project review looks at the process by which the system was written and makes recommendations for future projects. A hard look at the project plan should be revealing.

- Was the system changed after the systems proposal or systems specification were agreed? If so,
  - when and why did this happen;

- which phases of the project were affected;
- how much rework was required;
- what effect did this have on deadlines?

- Was the project completed on time and within budget? If not, how much extra time or money was needed?

- Was each phase completed on time? If any phase was late, did this mean that work was rushed in order to meet a deadline?

- What difficulties were encountered during development? Were they anticipated? Should they have been? How was the project affected?

- If a package was used as part of the system, to what extent do reported problems relate to it? This should include:

  - quality of documentation training;
  - response time and ease of use;
  - accuracy, timeliness and usefulness of data?

  Before finding fault with the package, the evaluation should be considered to see if the causes of complaint were dealt with in it.

- Were there any difficulties in combining the system with other systems and processes? To what extent was this due to the fact that an applications package was used?

- Was a prototype used? If so, did any problems occur in developing it and evaluating it?

- Were the results of the prototype evaluation introduced successfully into the system? Did the users fully understand what was happening?

- Were all the quality reviews and inspections laid down in the project or quality plan actually carried out? Does this have a bearing on any of the problems which have been reported?

- Was the project interrupted by any other work which meant that project staff were required to divert their efforts to other systems?

- Were there any staffing problems, e.g. recruitment, lack of suitable experience?

- Was training by external companies provided on time and to our satisfaction?

- Were all new software and hardware products provided on time? Did they live up to our expectations? Could they be used as easily and effectively as we believed?

- Was there any difficulty in obtaining user agreement to any part of the system? If so, why was this and what effect did it have on the project, for example, delays, rework?

- Were users always available when they were supposed to be, i.e. as they agreed when the project was planned?

- Were there any difficulties in communicating with users or the representatives of other companies? Why did this happen?

- Was cooperation within the computer department satisfactory? If not, what were the reasons?

- What aspects of the project went particularly well? Look for activities completed on time and assess the reasons for success. Some of the questions given above may provide clues. If the detailed systems analysis was an outstanding success was this perhaps partly due to the fact that a user with the right aptitude and knowledge was able to spend a lot of time with the systems analyst? If the project was on time because the team could be sufficiently well trained in a new software product within a short space of time, why not recommend that the same training company should be used in future?

Many of the questions above concentrate on possible problem areas. However, as the last question emphasises, the report should not only be concerned with showing what could have been done better. Positive feedback should always be encouraged as it can also serve elsewhere. Consider the example given in the last question. If the user had been trained in the same methodology as the project team and was therefore able to assist in the review of diagrams, why not recommend that other user departments should do the same?

Review

The review of both of the documents produced during this phase will look for recommendations for improvements. The documents should not merely sum up what went well and what did not. They should provide positive guidance for action. If the system is not performing well, the users will rightly expect it to be made to work properly. In addition, though, longer term considerations should be a high priority It is all too easy to lose sight of them because of more urgent demands on the systems manager's time. This can all too easily lead to the unwary repeating their mistakes.

Post-implementation system review

- Are all the assertions supported with clear, factual evidence?

- Is the report based on all the source, recommended above? If some have been omitted, what reason is given?

- Has the system been operational for long enough for the investigation to be able to draw conclusions about its benefits?

- Have any parts of the system not been considered? If so is there good reason for this? For example, annual processing may not yet be due.

- Are there any contradictions between the different sources, perhaps with some user, complaining about a feature of the system which others praise? If so, is a reason for this given in the report?

- Has the report investigated all the reasons for the defects?

- Is there anything to suggest that any of the defects have a common origin or belong to one process or facility of the system?

- Does the report recommend remedies for all the defects or any other changes to improve the system? Are they realistic, feasible and not out of the question because of cost?

- Does the report indicate any time constraints in implementing changes to the system?

- Were any of the defects foreseen as possible during the development? If so, why was nothing done about them? Time and cost constraints are possible reasons.

- Does the report make it clear how each defect arose and during which phase of the life cycle?

- Does the report point to any failings in the project team's dealings with users or other companies? If so, are the recommendations for action reasonable and likely to make for better systems in the future?

- Do any of the findings indicate that the user department is not making the best use of the system, with possible adverse consequences? How can this be remedied?

- Do any of the defects point to poor quality hardware or software? If so, does the report make a recommendation about what should be done?

- Do any of the findings or recommendations imply possible changes elsewhere, in other systems or in working practices, standard security procedures, etc?

- What aspects of the system are praised? Is there good reason for this?

- Does the report seek to blame individuals for any of the defects? If so, these remarks should be exercised.

Post-implementation project review

- Does the report make use of all the sources recommended above? Is a sound reason given if any have been omitted?

- Are all the assertions supported with clear, factual evidence?

- Does the report suggest that training is needed?

- What do we need to do, if anything, in order to ensure that user involvement is more fruitful in future?

- If the report points to any particular failings during the development, could they have been avoided? If so, what could have been done to avoid them?

- Did this project introduce any working practices not used previously by this department? How did they fare?

- If the report highlights any areas of particular achievement during the development, what were the reasons?

- What general lessons can be learnt about the way development projects are run? Consideration should be given to methodologies, planning, development software, standards, working practices and procedures, staffing levels, communications, etc.

- Are any individuals singled out? If so, remove these references.

End of phase

This phase will be judged complete when the reports have been read, considered and decisions taken as to what action is appropriate. The reports should not be shelved even if not all of the recommendations can be implemented. Something should be done about all of the recommendations even if it is only to reject them or to postpone them. In that way, at least there is some commitment to making longer term improvements.

- The report on the post-implementation system review has been discussed with all interested parties.

- The recommendations of the post-implementation system review have been accepted or rejected and the implementation of those accepted has been planned.

- The report on the post-implementation project review has been discussed with interested parties and its recommendations either implemented or rejected.

- The longer term implications of both have been considered by the computer department and plans to act on them have been made.

Appendix 1
Evaluating applications packages

The place of evaluations in the life cycle has been discussed above, mainly in Chapters 3 and 4. It is an integral part of systems development with packages being one way of fulfilling some or all of the requirements. Packages differ from 'in-house' development in two very important ways. They are designed to suit most people's needs so, even with a good package, you will need to take account of the difference between the full range of your requirements and the facilities on offer. They are also someone else's product, therefore the process of evaluating, implementing and maintaining the new system will depend to some extent on the manufacturer or supplier.

The first of these two points has been largely addressed in the life cycle chapters. If the package does not match all your requirements completely, there will be some processing which will be the subject of your normal, 'in-house' development. However, there is another option, perhaps the manufacturer will customise the package for you or even modify the package so that all other customers will benefit from your request. As for the second point, you need to satisfy yourself that the package does what it is supposed to do at reasonable cost, that it can be installed and introduced to the users without difficulty and that it will be maintained as long as you want to use it.

Take the example of a payroll, one of the most commonly used type of packages. There are so many on the market that it may be difficult to get a shortlist of suitable candidates. The reason for this is simple: a payroll is generally quite straightforward with everybody in the same country having to observe the same laws about taxation, social security, maternity benefits, sick pay and so on. Your choice will therefore be affected by other considerations. When rates for various deductions and benefits change or when the laws themselves change, a good manufacturer will provide updated software as soon as it is required. How do you know that you can rely on the manufacturer to do this? The best testimony is the word of a satisfied customer who will let you know how easy or difficult it was to learn about and install the package. You will learn about pitfalls from first hand experience.

Then you may have some special requirements: which of the packages you know about will do the processing you require? Some companies have bonus schemes which are so convoluted that some payrolls cannot cope with them. Give the details to a manufacturer and ask for a demonstration that a product will do what you want in a way which will be acceptable to your users. If you are offered customisation, will the manufacturer write it in such a way that further costly maintenance will not be needed?

So, you will have a number of questions to ask which go beyond the basic requirements and which start from the need to provide at least as high a level of quality as you would wish to achieve with an 'in-house' development (*see* Figure A1.1). The checklists given below have been drawn up with these points in mind.

QUESTIONS FOR THE SUPPLIER/MANUFACTURER

The Company

First, you need to be sure that a company is viable, that it is not likely to go bankrupt and that it has the resources to provide a quality product.

- How long have you been trading, both worldwide and in this country?
- How many staff do you employ both locally and throughout the world?
- Can you provide a copy of your latest annual report and statement of accounts?
- Is the product under evaluation designed, manufactured and maintained by you? If not, who is responsible?

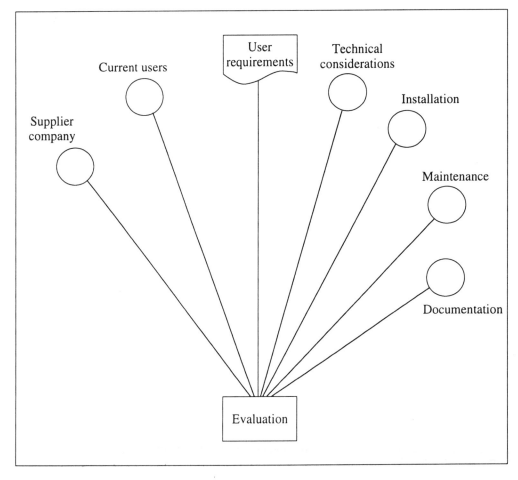

Figure A1.1   Types of questions in the evaluation

- Is your company registered for quality under ISO 9000? If not, what guarantees of the quality of the product can you offer? ISO 9000 is not a perfect guarantee but it shows commitment.

If the supplier is not the original manufacturer, it is worthwhile finding out about the latter, especially if your supplier is essentially a sales organisation. Perhaps the manufacturer is planning to discontinue the product.

The product

- How many customers do you have for this product?

- Have you any customer evaluations?

- Is there an independent user group?

- Will you customise the product if requested? If so,

   - will it be documented and supported;

   - will it be maintained whenever the product is amended or enhanced;

   - have you experience of customisation and the resources to do it;

   - how do you charge for it;

   - who owns the rights to the customised software?

- Is it possible for users to customise it in any way, for example by creating their own tables or reports? Taking the payroll example again, it should be possible to create some fairly straightforward payments and deductions of your own.

- Can the package be integrated with other systems and processes, including security arrangements?

- Is the data readily accessible for extraction by other processes?

- Is the product covered by an Escrow agreement? This will allow you to have the code for the product if the company goes bankrupt – not always as useful as it might seem.

- What standard contracts or licences do you use, both for the product and for maintenance?

- How has the product been improved over the last year?

- What enhancements are currently being developed?

- On what computers and with what operating systems can your product be used? Specify the versions.

- With what software and systems can your product interface?

- Will you ensure that the product works with the current range of machines, operating systems, etc. when they are upgraded by their manufacturers? If so, will payment be required?

- What is the minimum hardware configuration for the product?

- What are the maximum number of uses for the product?

- What volumes of data can the product handle?

- What language is the product written in?

- Does the product require any additional products to function properly, for example, software or hardware?

- What are the weak points of your product?

- Which is its closest rival and why? In what ways is yours a better product? This is a good way of finding out Just how interested the supplier really is in the market for the package.

- Is there a detailed functional description of your product?

- Which of our requirements can your product meet well and which might be more difficult (e.g. in terms of user convenience)?

- Which of requirements can be met only after modifying your product? What are your plans to do so? A salesman may not be well-informed about planned developments, may not fully understand the differences and similarities between your needs and the product and may want to get a sale without being overconcerned.

- Which of our requirements will be met by enhancements actually under development now? Even these should be taken with a pinch of salt since priorities change and some enhancements prove difficult or costly to introduce.

- When will promised enhancements and current enhancements which meet our requirements actually be met?

Installation and support

- When will the product be available?

- Are copies available for evaluation? If so,

  - what limitations does the evaluation version have;

  - what is the cost;

  - what special terms are required?

- If evaluation copies are not available, how do you recommend that customers assess the package? Manufacturers have problems with evaluation copies which are never returned but you nevertheless need to evaluate the product yourself. If there is no way of doing this, it should count very strongly against the package.

- How long does it take to install and become fully operational? This should include any data transfers from old systems, setting up data and training.

- Who will install it? What are the respective roles of the computer department, users and the supplier?

- What has to be done when the product is installed?

- What training is needed and when is it normally provided?

- How much training is provided as part of the original costs and what are the fees for any subsequent training?
- If formal courses are part of normal training, how often are courses normally organised?
- What site support is provided? If on-site assistance is needed, how long will it take for you to send someone?
- Is there a help desk for answering technical and user queries and is it in the same time zone?
- How long does it take to deal with a query? Do you have guaranteed response times?
- Does, the system have its own on-line 'help' subsystem?
- Is it fully documented for both users and computer staff and is this documentation kept up to date?
- Can the product be moved to another machine without the supplier's intervention?
- How do you supply new versions?
- If hardware provided as part of the package needs maintenance:
  - does it have to be returned to the supplier;
  - is it then sent elsewhere (e.g. abroad);
  - are replacements available *pro tem*?

Costs

- What is the current price and what do we get for this in terms of:
  - the basic product, including additional hardware or software needed to run it;
  - documentation;
  - upgrades;
  - training;
  - warranty;
  - maintenance?
- Thereafter, what are the charge, for upgrades, maintenance, additional training and documentation?
- Is there an escalation clause in the maintenance agreement?

Security

- What are the security features and what are they supposed to achieve?
- Is it possible for a designated user to administer access rights?
- Is an audit trail available?

- Can we log transactions?
- Should the system fail, e.g. because of a problem in the power supply:
  - what facilities for recovery are there;
  - how long will recovery take;
  - what happens to transactions being processed at the time of the failure?
- Can business controls still be used effectively with this product? For example, does it still preserve divisions of responsibility?
- If a breach of security occurs, will it provide enough information to provide evidence for a court of law?
- Is it possible that users could create data in contravention of data protection legislation?
- Does the package mean that any of the following will not be controlled by the computer department:
  - backup and recovery;
  - access control, including access to networks?
- What alterations to the working practices of the user department might be necessary if the product is installed and will this be detrimental to security?
- Are the controls at least as good as those currently used in the user department?

The last two question might be dealt with as part of the requirements as would most security considerations. They are included here since it is quite likely that the package will require some new working practices on the part of the users and these should be compared with the current situation.

QUESTIONS FOR CURRENT USERS OF THE PRODUCT

It is very useful to discover how others react to the product and a visit to another site should be most illuminating. The supplier should be able to arrange a visit.

Representatives of computer operations and users should be included on a site visit. Make sure that the people who will actually be doing the donkey work of using the system are included. They will be able to communicate with their peers and find out about the real joys and sorrows of using the package, often in casual conversation as much as by asking direct questions. These checklists will supplement the dialogue.

Questions for users

- Did the product match your expectations? In what ways were you disappointed and in what ways were you exceptionally pleased?
- What features do you like and dislike about the system?
- How long have you been using the product? Have you experienced all its features, including year end processing?

- Is there anything which the product cannot do which you would like it to do? Did you request this as an enhancement and, if so, what was the reaction of the supplier?
- What defects did you find? How serious were they?
- How long did it take to remedy any defects? Were you ever seriously inconvenienced by any defects?
- Did you learn about the product easily? Are any parts difficult to use? If so, do you still use them?
- Is help and advice easy to obtain? Do you make use of the 'official' helpdesk facility or of a personal contact?
- Did the supplier become less helpful after the product was purchased?
- Do the security features actually work? Is it more convenient to ignore them, assuming it is possible to do so?
- Would you rather work the way you did before acquiring the product?
- If you are doing the same job as before, does it take you more or less time?

Questions for the computer department

Some, of course, are the same as those for users.

- Why did you choose this product?
- What advantages did it have over others you considered?
- Did it meet all of your requirements? If not, how did you make up for this?
- In what ways has the product exceeded your expectations or fallen short of them?
- When you purchased the product, was your decision based on any promise about new facilities, for example, as part of an upgrade? If so, were the facilities provided?
- If the manufacturer states that new features will be added to the product, are such promises realised?
- With the benefit of hindsight, would you choose the same product again if you were evaluating now?
- Are you considering replacing the product and, if so, why?
- What defects did you discover? Were they serious? If so:
  - to what extent was processing disrupted;
  - has it been possible to rectify them to your satisfaction;
  - how long did it take to rectify them;
  - how much effort did it require of you and the users;
  - how supportive was the supplier?
- In general, has the supplier been helpful and prompt in dealing with inquiries?

- When the product needed to be upgraded, was this done on time and with minimal inconvenience to you and your users?

- If customisation was provided, has it been satisfactory, including maintenance of the customised features?

- How long have you been using the product for? Have you been through the complete cycle of processing?

- Was the documentation sufficient to enable you to run the system without having to ask the supplier for advice?

- Did installation give you any serious problems? Was it easy to transfer data from your old system?

- Has the product been fully compatible with other systems you run?

- Was the training adequate? Did it provide you with enough knowledge to be able to use the system with confidence?

- Have any problems occurred as a result of poor documentation, e.g. misinterpretation of an ambiguous statement?

- Has the product increased your workload when compared with the system it replaced? Consider regular operational procedures as well as intervention when users had problems or defects were discovered?

- Do you consider the product and the service you have received have given you value for money?

- Has any extra expenditure been required above your original expectations? If so, was it reasonable and justified?

- Did you have any security problems after you installed the package? How were these problems discovered and what countermeasures did you take?

These checklists presuppose that the product seems to offer a solution to your requirements and that you have evaluated it against them – see Chapter 3. Not every single question will apply in all cases. However, you will be concerned about the quality of the product and the service provided by the supplier for, unlike an 'in-house' system, neither is under your control. A conscientious supplier will understand your reasons for asking searching questions and will help you with arranging A visit to a user site.

It goes without saying that the evaluation should include practical experience of the system with the assistance of the supplier. You should make sure it works for you. Most responsible manufacturers will be happy to provide you with the means of doing so. You and your users can then see how your requirements are met in practice. You will only do this when the choice has been narrowed down to a very few candidates so it is in the interests of the supplier to cooperate.

Appendix 2
Managing Change

How is it possible to keep track of changes to documents? After a document has been reviewed it will probably be altered in some way. This may mean that documents which use it as a source will also have to be changed. What is more, the change may not only apply to the document in hand and its successors, perhaps the document from which it derived al so has to be modified.

The same is true even years after a system has been implemented when the project team has been disbanded. A change could mean a new systems development project, typically an extension of the system. More often, it will be because of new thinking about the detailed processing of the current system, the correction of an error or the result of external factors such as a change in the law. The systems development manager will decide whether or not the change warrants a new project but, generally, if it is not something additional but a change to the way we achieve the original aims of the system, it will be considered an amendment.

The first step towards effective change management is to identify each version of all documents. They should as a matter of course be identified at least by author and the date of issue. In addition, it is helpful to have some kind of version number as well, especially if the document is likely to be issued in more than one version. This is true of all key documents. Therefore, whenever a key document is changed, even if very slight, it should be re-issued with a new version number and date. For documents such as program specifications which tend to be changed quite frequently, it is useful to include an amendment history as well, showing what has been changed and when. In the case of program specifications, the version numbers of the specifications should be the same as those of the coding.

Urgent changes have to be treated as such but, even if you decide you have to cut corners, all documentation should be brought up to date as soon as the emergency is over. Making changes 'on the fly' and then putting them behind you as soon as possible without following the changes through will only create more problems.

The actual process of altering documents is relatively easy so long as a consistent policy is observed regarding choice of wordprocessing software, desktop publishing software and CASE tools. The invention of the word processor means that there is no excuse for the lazy way out of issuing a string of amendments and attaching them to the original document. This is still done with some program specifications. Reading becomes very difficult and mistakes are easily made. If a document is re-issued, it helps to highlight the changed part of the text in some way. You can point the reader to the changes in an introduction. The altered text can be clearly shown by using annotation in the margin or by a different typeface.

This appendix deals with two situations: change within a systems development project and change after the project has been implemented.

CHANGES DURING SYSTEMS DEVELOPMENT

If change during a systems development project is not properly controlled, serious errors of consistency can easily occur. Even a simple change such as the addition of a new data item or the way a data item is used can have unexpected repercussions. What if new data refers to a live person or if data about somebody is going to be accessed in a new way? Perhaps you need to think about compliance with data protection legislation.

Checklists are given here which deal with the two stages of change management: analysing the implications of the change and planning how to implement it.

Analysing the change

- Which documents, especially key documents, are affected by the change?

- Is the change feasible in view of current resources, skills, software, etc?

- Has the change been properly analysed? Does it need further research in order for us to appreciate the full implications?

- Has the request been authorised? It should have the written consent of the user responsible for liaison with the project team.

- Does the change imply any other changes, either to this program or others?

- Does the change contradict any other changes currently under consideration?

- Can the change be made at the same time as any others under consideration?

- Are there any contradictions or clashes between this change and any other processing in the system, where the latter is not being changed?

- Are the data structures, items or access paths affected in any way?

- Will the change affect other systems?

- Does the change imply that data from external sources such as another system will have to be modified before our system can be altered?

- Does the change refer to packaged software?

- Are there any legal or security implications, for example, does it appear to require extra security provisions or to reduce the level of security in any way?

- Will the performance of the system be affected by the modification? If so, will this mean that an agreed level of service might no longer be met?

Planning the change

- Does the change affect the current phase of the life cycle only? If not, how does it affect completed phases and which documents will have to be altered?

- How will the change affect planning for this and future phases of the project?

- Which documents in the current phase have been completed and will have to be revised?

- Which documents in the current phase are being worked on and will need revision? How much extra work will be needed?

- Will other documents have to be produced, for example, if the security implications make a business impact analysis necessary?

- What are the implications for the projected completion date of the system?

- What are the implications for the current phase, i.e. workload, tasks, time, staff and completion date? Do not forget that staff may have to revise work on early phases before completing their current tasks.

- What are the implications for earlier phases in terms of workload, tasks and time?

- What testing will he needed? Can it be limited to the program being altered or will other parts of the system, or even the whole system, need additional testing?

- What are the implications for quality? Does the change mean that reviews will have to be repeated?

- Would it be possible to complete and implement the system before making the change? If so, would it be advantageous to do so? This is most likely if the system is near completion and some benefit can be obtained from the system even without the amendment. It should be listed in a register of changes and given a priority number.

- Are the changes so extensive that it would be easier to abandon the project and begin again?

- If the changes require modification to other systems, when can they be made? How will this affect completion of this project?

- If the changes imply modification to packaged software, will the supplier make the change and, if so, when? What can be done if the supplier is reluctant?

The revised plan must address such matters as making sure that programs are tested again and that the test plans are revised to reflect the change.

CHANGES AFTER IMPLEMENTATION

The situation is slightly easier once the system has been implemented since both it and its documentation are now fixed. You no longer face the problems encountered during systems development when uncompleted documents may or may not be affected by a change. Nor will so many documents be affected since only the key documents will be kept up to date.

Obviously it is advantageous to make as many changes to the same documents at the same time. This is not always possible because of priorities but careful planning will identify opportunities for doing so.

Although the project has been finished, the structure of the life cycle has to be considered when making amendments. If a change affects the systems specification, it is likely to affect one or more program specifications, test plans, test data, program coding, user and operational documentation. Whoever is responsible for maintenance will have to trace the amendment back to the first key document and then forward again through all the subsequent phases. This is not as time consuming as it sounds so long as the documents are all current.

Simple errors do not always need to be treated like this. If a program contains an error, i.e. it does not do something the specification says it should do, only the coding needs to be corrected and tested. It is worthwhile showing such changes on the program listing as part of the amendment history but distinguish them from requested changes which imply a specification change as well. If you use version numbers, a correction should be treated as a 'version within a version', subordinate to the numbering used for requested changes. However, if the error originated earlier in the life cycle, for example if a data item has been created which is not the size it should be, you will obviously have to go back to the first document which was in error and trace it forward.

The following assumptions made about change management procedures in the checklists given below.

- There are established channels of communication for making requests for changes and only authorised people can request them.

- The systems have been developed using a life cycle or other formal approach and that documentation is sufficient.

- All maintenance is carried out by a maintenance team.

- All requests for changes are logged in a register where they are classified according to urgency and grouped together if they affect the same parts of the system.

Analysing the change

- Is this a request for a modification to the system or does it point to an error in the system? If it is the latter, consider:
  - what parts of the system are affected by it;
  - was the error made by the systems development project team or is it external, for example, a software error, an error in an applications package;
  - is it urgent or can it be lived with for the time being?

  The last point is made because it is sometimes worth combining the correction of an error with other planned changes.

- When does the change have to be made? Generally speaking, three categories are sufficient:
  - urgent – to be done as soon as possible;
  - date-related – to be done by a specific date;
  - non-urgent – can wait until more pressing work has been finished.

- Has the request been properly authorised?

- Is it clear precisely what is required? Is there any reason for doubting that the user understands the full implications of the change and not just the immediate results?

- Does it affect only 'in-house' applications or does it extend to other systems outside the control of the computer department, applications package, etc?

- Is the nature of the change such that it should be considered a new subsystem?

- Is there an adequate test environment? Remember that in general not only the programs being altered will need to be tested.

- Does the maintenance team have sufficient expertise to make the change and, if not, when can the expertise be made available?

- Is the documentation software used in the development of the system available to the maintenance team?

- Which life cycle documents that have to be kept up to date are affected by the change?

- Does the change imply any other changes, for example to linked systems?

- Does the change contradict any other changes currently under consideration?

- Can the change be made at the same time as any others under consideration?

- Are there any contradictions or clashes between this change and any other processing in the system, where the latter is not being changed?

- Are there any legal or security implications, for example does it appear to require extra security provisions or to reduce the level of security in any way?

- Will the performance of the system be affected by the modification? If so, will this mean that an agreed level of service might no longer be met?

- Are the data structures, items or access paths affected in any way?

- What information needs to be conveyed to quality assurance staff, for example, for their records of defect detection?

Planning the change

- Are there any data management requirements, i.e. where data structures have to be altered? When will the revised data structures be available?

- When will staff be available to make the change? If there are insufficient staff, could the use of contractors be considered?

- If there is any need for training for development staff, when can it be completed?

- What are the workloads and completion dates for each activity? List all the activities and documents which are affected.

- Which staff will be responsible for each activity?

- When will the work be complete?

- When will the work be implemented?

- If there is a deadline for the work, is there any serious risk of this not being met? What would the implications be?

- Are reviews needed? If so, when will they be held and who will attend them?

- Will the work mean that training will be needed for users or operations staff? If so, who will provide the training and when?

- When will the implementation plan be ready? This should be discussed with computer operations. A detailed implementation plan may not be needed if the changes only affect one or two programs. Even so, it is advisable to plan a suitable time for implementation, making sure that system's data will not be corrupted. At the very least, computer operations should be given as much warning as possible of what new or amended programs will be handed over and when so that they can fit it in with their other work.

- Who else needs to be told about the changes?

- If the changes make modification of other systems necessary, when can this be done? Will this adversely affect the deadline for the work?

- If the changes imply modification to packaged software, when will this be completed?

- What testing is needed? Is a full system test required?

- What documents have to be changed? Consider in particular:

    - program specifications;

    - user documentation;

    - operations documentation;

    - the system specification.

It is important to check that the changes to documentation are actually made.

Reading difficult documents

READING BETWEEN THE LINES

One of the reasons why the first phase of a systems development project is most prone to error is that the project team may be working from documents which are either very poor or else simply not intended as a source document. for a computer systems development. This is especially true if the project manager has been asked to look at the requirements for a completely new area where computers have never been used before. Written office procedures and manuals may help you find out about what is happening now but they may be outdated and leave gaps which are not a problem for those who know the job, but are for others.

Similarly, a user request may be written down, but not in terms which can be readily translated into a statement of requirements. The request may turn up as a short memorandum with an internal report attached to it. The memorandum may only state that the department has been thinking of computerisation for some time and that someone wrote a report on it which sums up the departmental manager's views. Frequently it will only deal vaguely with what you are looking for. It might say that such-and-such an improvement is needed without looking at what has to be done to make it possible and without stating why the improvement would be beneficial.

Faced with such a document, you will obviously have a number of questions to ask the user department: you should also ask questions of the document. This means not accepting the content at face value but reading between the lines, getting a clear idea of the circumstances in which the document was written and interpreting it in the light of other sources of information. The latter may include other documents, interviews and discussions with users and knowledge of the current capabilities of computer systems. While most of us are familiar with users who would like a computer to perform function, requiring telepathy, there are many who do not appreciate just how much a computer can actually do.

So, a request needs interpretation, not least if it is written in terms of what the user thinks the computer should do. We need to ask: what really is the problem you want to solve? When we know that, we can start worrying about a solution. What questions should we ask? Below are some which might be useful. Similar questions are used in a variety of disciplines, especially history, as a means of finding out the significance of the written word.

What type of document is it?

Are we looking at a document which has a direct bearing on the subject? Let us say a department has expressed an interest in putting its card files onto a computer system, what bearing does this document have on the subject? Does it state what the department hopes to achieve? An example of a misleading document which is meant to be helpful would be one which states, "We have read about computers which can have card files on them. We have got card files going back for twenty years and we want to put them on a computer. Can you give us a computerised card filing system?" Of course, the request tells you nothing about the problem. It is an attempt to provide a solution without first analysing the need.

Other types of document, such as internal reports, may also fall into this category or they may tell you what is the current situation without saying why there is a problem with it. In other words, it may be obvious, that the situation is not satisfactory but the author has not looked further and identified what needs to be achieved.

When was it written?

Documents quickly become outdated. It is important that it should be as close in time as possible to the topic under investigation. Even with documentation produced by a computer department, you may be trying to find out what an old system did without realising that it has changed over the years. Alternatively, the documentation may accurately tell you that the system is much as it was originally written – but what of the actual use of the system? Sometimes a whole subsystem is written at the insistence of a manager, After this manager leaves, the next one may not require it and never touch it.

However good a document may be, it may no longer be relevant. A comparison with actual practice is important, especially if the document is not recent.

Who wrote it?

Is the author someone who you would expect to have in-depth knowledge of the topic? A senior manager may have clear ideas about his own needs but little knowledge about the workings of the department which gives him his data. His perception of the function of the department may be clouded by the service it provides him. Perhaps he is jumping to conclusions and we need to delve further to understand all the implications of the request.

Why was it written?

Beware of being asked to glean something useful from a document written for a different purpose, for example, an expensive report written by consultants on a different subject.

Even if the document is a request for a system, the reasons for making it may be illuminating. A statement such as "we want to put our records on the computer because we are always talking to customers on the phone and can never get hold of the information we want" tells you two obvious facts: locating and retrieving record, need to be faster. Is that all? What has made this an issue now – customer complaints, staff complaints or the hope that the computer will save the user manager's neck? Perhaps some other aspects of the way the department does its work need to be considered. A closer examination might reveal that records are inaccurate, contain superfluous information or need to be supplemented by data from elsewhere. You know there is a problem, you know what the user manager thinks is the reason for the problem but other factors should be considered. A sketchy request like this one, without any statistical evidence, should not be taken at face value.

Who was it written for?

The people who were intended to read may make certain assumptions which you do not know about. Within a department, all may be familiar with a way of doing things or a reference to a source of information of which you are unaware. The author will take things for granted.

What does the document tell you?

It might set out to tell you something, but look for unwitting testimony as well. Take the example above. of the card file with records going back for twenty years. Sometimes records are needed for much longer than that but, even so, twenty years is a long time. Could it be that redundant records are never scrapped or filed away somewhere else? With your knowledge of the department's business you will probably have a good idea. At all events, you will have questions to ask.

How will the target readers understand the document?

Let us say one user writes to another user with a complaint about the way an old computer system works. You are given a copy and, with your knowledge, you can read between the lines and see what the real problem is. Perhaps it is not the computer system *per se* but new expectations on the part of the user. This is all very well but when you come to reply you need to ask yourself why have expectations changed and also to address the concerns which the other users may share and will almost certainly accept at face value.

This is a very useful question to ask of your own work as well.
These questions will rarely provide solutions by themselves. They should help you decide what you need to ask next.

AMBIGUITY

Ambiguity was considered in Chapter One in the discussion on the General Purpose Checklist as something which should always be looked for when you are reviewing a document. There is no easy way of dealing with ambiguity. It is especially difficult for the author of a document to spot. simply because the author knows what he or she means. A review will be more likely to discover ambiguity and it may well be worthwhile asking one of the reviewers to concentrate on this particular defect. How many ways can a sentence be read? Does the context make the meaning clear or does it only add to the confusion?

There follows a few examples of ambiguity. They are the sort of statements which are often found in computer documentation such as program specifications where great care is needed. The examples focus on a few words which (apart from 'billion') often give trouble. In the context in which these statements are going to be read and interpreted, they are all open to at least two interpretations. Think in terms of communicating with a machine which is what the programmer will soon have to do anyway.

You may well think of other interpretations in addition to those given here. If so, that is a testimony to the benefits of painstaking review.

After

Quantity will be displayed after sales value.

- Quantity will be displayed immediately after sales value.

- Quantity will be displayed somewhere after sales value.

All

All transaction records are linked to a master file record.

- A single master file links all transaction records.

- There are a number of master file records each of which is linked to a single transaction record.

- There are a number of master file records each of which is linked to one or more transaction records.

Billion

The maximum value for this field is a billion.

- The maximum value for this field is 1,000,000,000.

- The maximum value for this field is 1,000,000,000, 000.

You may laugh at the last example and say that for years nobody has used 'billion' when they mean 1,000,000,000,000. It is certainly true that the use of 'billion' for 1,000,000,000 is now almost universal. The last time I saw it with the 'million million' meaning (admittedly not in a computer context) was in 1987 which is not so long ago. It is not likely to cause you any problems but you never know. Expressing numbers with figures rather than words should make for absolute clarity. If you want to be pedantic you could always try to resurrect 'milliard' but do not be surprised if nobody knows what you are talking about.

Both

Both records are controlled by a master file record.

- A single master file record controls both records.

- Each record is controlled by a master file record which may or may not be the same one.

Following

The sales value is on the following record with an identity code of 'S'.

- The sales value is on the next record and that record will have an identity code of 'S'.
- The sales value will be on the next record which has an identity code of 'S'. It may or may not be the record which immediately follows this one.

Last

Move the sales total to the last record.

- Move the sales total to the last record of the file.
- Move the sales total to the last record read.

May

The field may contain a letter or a blank.

- The field must only contain either a letter or a blank.
- The field may contain a letter or a blank but it might contain something else.

Same

The sales and cost of sales records are the same.

- The sales record has the same format as the cost of sales record.
- The sales and cost of sales records have the same format as another type of record.

Should

The data element should be set to ZZZZZZZ.

- The data element should already be set to ZZZZZZZZ.
- The program should set the data element to ZZZZZZZZ.

Until

Count all records read until the last one.

- Count all records except the last one.
- Count all records including the last one.

When

Set the field to zero when the master file is read.

- Set the field to zero every time the master file is read.

- Set the field to zero the first time you read the master file.

This final example contains another potential cause of woe. Suppose that the field can contain a string of letters, characters or spaces. Does the author mean "fill the field with zeros" or "move a single zero to the field"? If the latter is meant should it be right- or left-justified, and what will the rest of the field contain?

Controls in systems development

You cannot have quality without security. A well-designed system, which does everything the user has asked for, is second-rate if its security is easily compromised – even if security was not one of the user's requirements. In the life cycle chapters, we examined how to investigate the impact of breaches of security and looked at ways of bringing security into the system so that the countermeasures will match the risk. Now there follows a section on designing controls, together with examples of some types of control. This Appendix will be of most use during the Definition and Design phases.

One point which must be made from the start: the best security measures are most effective if there is a high level of security awareness. Who has not heard stories of people writing their passwords on a piece of paper and attaching it to their PC? Clever technical controls will be of little use if they are not enforced. The feeling that once something is 'in the computer' it is safe still endures. Sometimes traditional controls such as the division of responsibilities are allowed to lapse. A manager may delegate some responsibilities to a member of staff without considering the possibility of misuse.

Security procedures should be well-defined so nothing is left to chance. An unused control, or one that is not used fully, gives a false sense of security. The advice of security experts should always be sought to ensure that controls are truly effective.

Designing controls

A control is an important part of any system and needs to be designed, tested and documented as well as any other process. This checklist assumes that the need for a control has been laid down as a requirement and that we have thought about its place in the system. The questions will be useful in documenting the control as a procedure, showing the role of people as well as the computer. Such documentation is part of the overall system documentation although it may be desirable to make some of it confidential.

What is the aim of control?

The source document should provide this information. It should be taken into consideration when the control is tested – does the control actually achieve what it set out to do in business as opposed to purely technical terms?

What activates the control?

The control may be activated by exceptional circumstances, such as an error or apparent breach of security. Others are part of everyday processing, perhaps double-checking the validation, and are automatic. Some require human intervention, for example some PC access control devices will only provide reports on password failures if you select an option on a menu. It is important to distinguish between these types of controls. If you find there is a preponderance of controls which are only invoked by deliberate human intervention, you may like to consider whether or not they will be used conscientiously enough to provide real security.

What is the relationship between this control and other security features of the system?

A full understanding of one control may depend on another. Thus, if a user's control report suggests that there are discrepancies between the number of records on an input file and the number of records written to a database, another report might need to be run in order to discover why. Alternatively, the user may be advised to contact the computer department in order to alert it to possible data integrity problems.

How should the control be interpreted?

The basic message of the control should be as clear as possible. Taking access control for example, assume a simple report on access highlighted the fact that a user apparently logged on at 2 a.m. for two hours. It is right to draw attention to this fact but what does it signify? The person reviewing the report should know what questions to ask next and what sources of information are available. In this case, perhaps the user is working abroad in another time zone and has good reason to want to use the system. Such possibilities should be checked before jumping to conclusions. Those responsible for checking controls should be trained to do so.

How does the control work?

The step-by-step functioning of the control must be made clear, showing what processing it is linked with and also what processing it must not be linked with. Controls should be independent, genuine and not produced by precisely the same process they are supposed to be controlling.

   A simple record count in a program is a useful means of assessing the success of the program and drawing attention to problems. Assume a program specification stated that a control report would show records read from a file, records updated to a database and records which had to be rejected for some reason. Let us say a lazy programmer counted the records being read, counted the number of rejects and calculated the number of records updated by subtracting the rejects from the records read from the input file.

---

1. A control report which does not control anything

   - Records read from file INSSOl   3000

   - Records updated to COSTBASE   2995

   - Records rejected   5

In this report, the total for records updated is produced by subtracting the records rejected from the records read (see text). We do not know how many records were really updated.

2. A genuine control report

   - Records read from file INSSOl   3000

   - Records updated to COSTBASE   2994

   - Records rejected   5

   - Total processed   2999

   Control Discrepancy – Total Processed Disagrees with Total Read

In the second example, the records updated have actually been counted. When added to the total rejected, the discrepancy with the total read is plain to see.

Figure A4.1   Control reports

This is not a genuine control – records which are updated are not counted so a failure in the updating process is not recorded. It is not only the programmer who is at fault, though. The specification should have stated that the total records read should be compared with the sum of the records rejected and records updated and any discrepancy highlighted on the report. Otherwise the control is not independent and is produced by the same processes it is supposed to control (*see* Figure A4.1).

What should be done especially if further action is indicated?

The person checking the control should be trained to know what to do both if something might be wrong or if all appears to be in order. If a control report shows that all is well, it might be worthwhile keeping it until the next time the report is run. In the case of a possible breach of access control security of the type given above, the procedure might be to keep a record of all such records even when an innocent explanation is offered.

Perhaps someone logs-on late on Thursday evening to do some extra work. This is repeated over the next few months – is he really that conscientious? Perhaps a quiet word with his manager might be in order. If it happens when he is supposed to be on holiday, we would be justified in wondering if all is as it seems. A good monitoring procedure will trap such patterns of behaviour.

What happens to output from the control?

All controls have some kind of output, even if it is only a display on a screen. Other output might be a file which can be interrogated or a printed report. It should be clear what should be done with the output, how long it should be kept and where, who can see it and to whom it should be communicated after initial interpretation.

An example of controls – monitoring transactions

One of the traditional controls of finance which can be brought into a computer system is the authorisation of transactions. This is essentially no more than a variation on the need to have two signatures on one cheque which is a well-established control, generally only used if large suns of money are involved.

Imagine that a company regularly sends orders to a large number of suppliers and that this is going to be handled by a new computer system. The possibility of fraud or error is obvious: what can the system do to prevent it?

In the first place, consider who authorises transactions at the moment. Typically, a supervisor has to countersign an order which has been drawn up by a member of staff. Why not keep this division of responsibilities in the system? Of course, there is the possibility of a conspiracy but, even so, there are ways of limiting this, for example by limiting the cost of the order and by making sure that the supervisor's own manager can monitor what is going on. The same control would limit honest errors, for example an extra zero accidentally added to the number of items being ordered. An experienced supervisor would be likely to spot such a mistake.

So, having decided on what sort of approach we are going to take, what do we need to ask ourselves in more detail in order to design some effective controls?

Who can initiate an order?

In this situation it would be any member of the Orders Department who has been given the appropriate facilities. This assumes that there will be a strict method of access control. Only those authorised to initiate orders should have the capability of doing so.

What can be ordered and from which companies?

The value of an order can be limited to a certain amount, to a quantity of goods or to types of goods. A masterfile of suppliers will also reduce the possibility of error or fraud. Exceptions would need exceptional processing.

Who can authorise orders?

Here it must be the supervisor, or someone else who can act as a deputy. Perhaps another supervisor or the departmental manager should be able to authorise when the supervisor is away. However, the supervisor should not normally be able to authorise his own orders.

How is authorisation requested?

Clearly, the supervisor has to be made aware that authorisation is needed so some form of communication has to be built in to the procedure or perhaps he will only authorise orders at certain times of day.

How is authorisation granted?

After checking the order, the supervisor should be able to write it to another file for the next stage of processing. After this, no alteration should be possible, except cancellation.

The system should make sure that the supervisor is able to access sufficient data to make sure the order is correct.

What evidence of the order will be preserved?

A file of all orders, showing who initiated them and who authorised them, would be kept for a predetermined period.

The amount of detail will depend on what you hope to achieve by the control. If, for example, you want to make sure you have enough evidence of any fraud to stand up in a court of law, you should design the output from the controls so that it will show exactly which individual has performed what function and when. This might have to be linked to other evidence from access control monitoring programs, for example, to show that so-and-so was indeed logged on to the computer when a transaction was made and that he then used the same terminal to log on as the supervisor and authorise the order.

What can be done to monitor this procedure?

The departmental manager should be able to review all orders independently, without having to inform anyone else. Regular control reports could highlight duplicate orders, others might show orders dispatched against orders authorised or orders received against orders requested, again with discrepancies highlighted.

Conclusions

This shows how much effort may be needed to develop effective controls. A business impact analysis will have told you if it is worthwhile and suggested the types of controls needed. Here we have considered controls relating to the integrity of the system. The example is not complete, the problem of deputising for the supervisor has not been dealt with fully. However, it has been identified as a potential problem which needs to be examined now. Otherwise, the temptation will be to find an insecure emergency solution which then becomes permanent.

These controls will be stronger if linked to others. Should the master file of suppliers be updated by the people making the orders if it allowed the possibility of a temporary change for fraudulent purposes? We should think about a division of responsibility or a report on all changes showing when and by whom they were made. If the orders were processed entirely electronically, security could be easily increased by matching records of orders dispatched records of receipt and processing from the destination system.

The creation of effective controls may be time-consuming but you cannot develop a true quality system without making sure that it does not fail because security has been skimped.

Security during the latter phases of the life cycle

The life cycle concentrated on discovering potential security problems at an early stage and then turning them into requirements. However, risks can be uncovered at any time. It may be necessary to conduct a business impact analysis and even to think through part of the system again. Often, though, controls can be included without having to backtrack.

An example is the use of suspense accounts or data structures which are set up to deal with exceptions to normal processing. These might be planned but are sometimes needed because a need was not identified earlier and there is no time now to rethink the system. The temptation is to think of them as of little interest to the system since they will probably not contain much data and are only of interest to one or two people. Therefore, security is not considered to be of great importance. Unfortunately, this is a gift to a potential fraudster.

Therefore, if you have to use something like a suspense account, make sure it is well managed. Check movements in and out, especially if large amounts of money are involved. Provide the manager with regular reports, drawing attention to what has been in there for a long time. Above all, make sure access is restricted and that transactions have to be properly authorised. If the structure is a last minute creation, put down that part of the system as something to be reconsidered after implementation.

Security within the system and installation standards

Security is made easier if some security standards already exist. In many computer installations the availability of systems is addressed by a disaster recovery policy which, if kept under review and updated when necessary, will enable systems to be restored should a major disaster occur. Copies of data are regularly made and stored in secure off-site locations where they can be used to recreate the data structures shortly before the disaster. With efficient logging and locking arrangements, the damage to a database caused by a sudden loss of power can be minimised because the log files can be used to recreate the data at the time of the loss of power, often after only a few minutes.

Such arrangements are normally standard for all users. They offer an agreed level of protection which suits everybody – regular reviews will make sure they remain current. Similar procedures are often used for access control. The computer department will give access rights to different systems at the request of the system owners. In addition, personal computers will have their own security device, normally a standard security package stopping anyone other than the PC's owner from using it.

Such common standards are beneficial to systems development since they offer a baseline against which the particular needs of a system can be measured. But they also can be a hindrance for two reasons. The first is that they give credence to the myth that security is not something which should concern systems development staff over much, in other words it is someone else's problem. The second is that it can represent a serious hurdle if the new system needs a level of security which is higher than normal.

In such circumstances, there are three things you can do.

- When the need has been identified, re-examine the current standard. Perhaps it is time to review it anyway. How important is the new system in relation to the others? If it is easier to upgrade the level of security for everyone than to make this system a special case, why not investigate further?

- Look for ways of using the current method in a different way. Take access control to a mainframe computer for example. Perhaps most users are happy with an arrangement whereby access rights are actually provided by the computer department at the request of the users. The manager of a new system has decided that this is not secure enough: he wants to control it himself. The method of granting access control rights on some mainframes is not exactly user friendly, requiring a knowledge of the operating system and possibly enabling the user to do other things which could actually cause security problems. Would it be impossible to give the manager only sufficient access to perform these functions, perhaps writing some programs to make it easier?

- Accept that special arrangements must be made for this system only and then calculate what it will cost and the additional workload it will entail. Is it still worthwhile in view of the benefits which will derive from the system?

In short, installation security standards are a factor to be considered when assessing security arrangements and will generally be very useful. They should not however be regarded as eternal, immutable laws.

Appendix 5

Creating your own quality checklists

While this book covers a range of documents, it cannot include every possible document which might be used in systems development project. Methodologies have their own documentation standards and individual companies have their own rules as well about form and content.

Designing your own checklists is not difficult so long as you observe a few simple principles. It has been stated above that you should adapt the checklists given in this book to suit your own needs. Why not take this one step further and create your own?

The first question to ask yourself is: what is the purpose of the checklist you want to design? In this book, two main viewpoints have been taken. The first is that of the person actually creating the document; the second is of those who review it. These overlap, indeed one of the questions the review can always ask is: has the author paid sufficient attention to the checklists, guidelines and standards which should be observed when creating the document?

The review also pays attention to where the individual document fits into the overall scheme of things, what its intended readers are likely to make of it, whether it is true to its sources and whether it contains any implications that go beyond its scope. So, the review is at once a detailed examination, seeing if the rules have been observed and if errors have been made, and a much broader perspective as well.

After that, consider what other checklists you have and whether or not you can adapt them. It would be rare indeed if you could not take some items from other checklists. For reviews, the general purpose checklist given in Chapter 1 can be adapted for many different types of document. Comparison with other documents should also be included, but try to work out just what you hope to achieve by the comparison and how relevant one document is to another. If you are comparing one document with a source document, do you want to insist that everything in your document must be derived from the source? It makes life simpler if you can impose a strict rule like this but there may be a very good reason for including something else.

When thinking up checklists for the authors of documents, avoid overemphasising form at the expense of content. This is not to say that presentation is unimportant but, if the content is not right, the form is irrelevant. Indeed, it may be misleading, some people are beguiled by well-presented rubbish. Some standards dwell entirely on presentation, the sort of standard which tells you the precise order of paragraphs in a system specification and which fonts to use for subheadings but does not remind the author about everything which has to be considered when writing about data. Form and presentation are aids to clarity and readability.

Checklists should ask questions: they are really no more than the questions the authors of a documents should be asking themselves and the questions reviewers should ask of the document in front of them. They should provoke thought and not be regarded as no more than a list of possible contents or things to look out for as in the case of auditors' checklists. Do not forget that the general-purpose checklist given in Chapter 1 can be adapted quite easily.

So, now for two simple checklists for designing checklists.

Designing a checklist for creating a document

This sort of checklist is generally quite straightforward and not always necessary. If the document is a standard methodology document where the rules for such a document are well defined, a checklist can be dispensed with. However, note the last item below since the level of detail of a diagram may be inappropriate.

- Is there already a good example of this sort of document which the author should emulate?

- What is the aim of the document?

- Who are its intended readers?

- Is there another kind of document which resembles this one and for which a checklist already exists? If so, can its checklist be adapted here?

- What rules, standards or guidelines should the author observe?

- What sources of information should the author consult?

- Should any documents be treated as source documents? If so, what should the relationship between this document and the source documents be? Should it be entirely derived from it?

- What is the scope of the document? What should be included in the contents? This should be considered in the light of the aim of the document and its place in the life cycle.

- Which of the contents are compulsory? State any subject the document must cover.

- What should the author be thinking about when writing this document? Every point should be the subject of a question in a checklist.

- If this is a methodology document, to what level of detail should it be taken at this stage?

Designing a checklist for reviewing a document

- What do we want to achieve by this checklist? Remember that you may be preparing for a review in which individuals look at the document from a different viewpoint and the checklist for each individual will only deal with what he or she is looking for.

- Is there another kind of document which resembles this one and for which a checklist already exists? If so, can its checklist be adapted here?

- How relevant is the general-purpose checklist (see Chapter 1) to this one? Can it be used intact or should it be adapted? The points in the general-purpose checklist about defect analysis are almost certainly valid. You should always check for things which are missing, wrong or superfluous.

- Has the author obeyed the rules and followed the guidelines for writing this sort of document?

- Has the document achieved its stated aim?

- Does it contain anything which requires further action? Include action outside the normal systems development process. For example, it may point to a security risk which has not been noticed before or may make clarification with another computer site necessary.

- Will the document make sense to all its intended readers?

- Is it suitable as a source document?

- Is it true to its sources?

- Is the scope of the contents appropriate for a document of this sort?

- What does the document not tell you that you think you ought to know about?

- Are there any contradictions within the document or between it and other documents?

- Are there any apparent contradictions between this document and others?

- If you are using a formal approach such as the Fagan Inspection Method, does the checklist tie in with the method? For example, defect codes are used in FIM so every defect code should be represented by a question in the checklist.

Review both kinds of checklist before issuing them for clarity, consistency and accuracy. It would be embarrassing to say the least if the checklists said one thing and your standards said another.

An example – a checklist for a user role/function matrix

Consider the user role/function matrix given in Figure 1.3. This is a very straightforward document enabling the reader to see at a glance which users perform which functions within a system. It is concerned with roles rather than individuals so, in the example in question, all sales staff perform the same roles.

This matrix can be used during different phases of the life cycle but is most useful from Definition onwards. Let us assume that Figure 1.3 has been developed as part of the System Proposal and that we want to review it. So as well as thinking of what questions we should ask of a user role/function matrix, is there anything which is unique to such a document when prepared during Definition?

First, though, the most obvious questions which we can ask are about the notation. SSADM has a fairly strict notation and uses standard forms. We can ask about both: is the form correct and has it been filled in correctly? This should include the boxes along the top of the form. SSADM allows you to enter an 'X' to show that a user can perform a function or 'C' to show that it is critical. So, there is no error here but we may have to ask ourselves why nothing critical has been identified.

Next, there is the question of the source. Where should we have got our information from? The answer will probably be the statement of requirements and we can therefore compare it with that document. We also know who does what in the department perhaps from an organisation chart. Depending on the project there may be other sources as well but the statement of requirements is a key document and there should at least be no contradiction between the matrix and the statement. Obviously the matrix will expand on what has been said in the requirements but it would probably be unacceptable if we invented a new position which does not exist and which was not part of the requirements.

At the same time we should look for consistency between the matrix and the system proposal, assuming it is part of the proposal, and any other SSADM document which has been used in it. If a dataflow diagram has been used it should show the same functions.

Presentation is mainly decided by the layout of the form but we might consider the people who are going to read it and ask what sense they will make of it, in this care it will include users. Will they be happy with the roles we have described and will they understand the functions we have defined?

Thinking about the use the project team will make of the document later on, how useful is it? Could it be used as a tool in deciding how the menu system should work?

Does the document tell us everything that we could reasonably expect from it? Going back to the question of marking critical functions with a 'C', should the author have done this? Perhaps it is not really complete. A 'C' can be used to show a number of things but mainly to make the readers sit up and take note. Users should be told if something is critical as a business function or if it represents a new way of doing things. The project team might like to know which functions are performed by many users, especially users who have a different perspective on the system, or those which are going to be used more frequently than others.

Finally, we should look at all the implications of the matrix. In Chapter 1, the point was made that it looked as though the system could grind to a halt if the warehouse manager went on holiday because nobody else would be checking the stock levels. This is a potential weakness in the system which should be dealt with now.

So, a checklist for our user role/function matrix would look something like this.

- Does the matrix conform to SSADM standards?

- Is it fully annotated?

- Does it match the source documents accurately?

- Does it match the system proposal and the LDS?

- Is it complete, showing all the user roles and functions for the system?

- Does it provide enough information to be used as a source document for subsequent phases?

- Does it imply any potential security problems?

- Does it provide enough information for all interested parties to make a decision about the future development of the system?

- Is there anything which needs to be expanded for clarity?

- Will it be understood by its intended readers?

There is no guarantee that the questions would draw the readers attention to any particular area which might need improvement. Review depends on human intelligence and the checklists can be no more than a stimulus to thought. However, different questions might focus on the same problem. With a number of reviewers all looking at the matrix from different standpoints, you are more likely to find matters which need to be re-examined. Here the identification of critical functions might be considered appropriate by someone thinking of the future use of the matrix in the life cycle, by a user with a knowledge of SSADM or someone concerned with security.

Bibliography

Crosby P. *Quality is Free*, McGraw-Hill, 1979

De Marco T, *Controlling Software Projects, Management, Measurement and Estimation*, Yourdon Press, 1982

De Marco T, *Structured Analysis and System Specification*, Prentice Hall, 1979

Fagan M E, Design and Code Inspections to Reduce Errors in Program Development, *IBM Systems Journal*, Vol. 15, No. 3, 1976

Gilb T, *Principles of Software Engineering Management*, Addison-Wesley, 1988

Grady R, Dissecting Software failures, *Hewlett-Packard Journal*, April, 1989

Hetzel, Bill, *The Complete Guide to Software Testing*, QED, 1988

Jackson M A, *Principles of Program Design*, Academic Press, 1975

Jackson M A, *Systems Development*, Prentice-Hall, 1983

Longworth G, *A User's guide to SSADM Version 4*, NCC Blackwell, 1982

National Centre for Software Engineering, *Framework for success: a guide to quality in software development and support*, National Centre for Software Engineering (Ireland), 1982

Ould M A, *Strategies for Software Engineering: the management of risk and quality*, Wiley, 1990

Paans R, Herschberg I S, Auditing the Change Management System, *Computers and Security*, No. 9, 1990

Perry, W E, *Effective Methods of EDP Quality Control*, QED, 1988

Sharland R, *Package evaluation: a practical guide to selecting applications and systems software*, Averbury Technical, 1991

Skidmore S, Farmer R, Mills G, *SSADM Version 4 Models and Methods*, NCC Blackwell, 1992

Skidmore S, Wroe E, *Introducing Systems Analysis*, NCC Blackwell, 1988

Skidmore S, Wroe E, *Introducing Systems Design*, NCC Blackwell, 1990

Smith M F, *Software prototyping: adoption, practice and management*, McGraw-Hill, 1991

Wood C C, Principles of Secure Information Systems Design, *Computers and Security*, No. 9, 1990

Yourdon E, *Modern Structured Analysis*, Yourdon Press, 1989

Index